Reflections

Maureen Garbarino

Note for Librarians: a cataloguing record for this book that includes Dewey Decimal Classification and US Library of Congress numbers is available from the Library and Archives of Canada. The complete cataloguing record can be obtained from their online database at:
www.collectionscanada.ca/amicus/index-e.html
ISBN 1-4120-4189-9
Cover painting by Maureen Garbarino

TRAFFORD

Offices in Canada, USA, Ireland, UK and Spain
This book was published *on-demand* in cooperation with Trafford Publishing. On-demand publishing is a unique process and service of making a book available for retail sale to the public taking advantage of on-demand manufacturing and Internet marketing. On-demand publishing includes promotions, retail sales, manufacturing, order fulfilment, accounting and collecting royalties on behalf of the author.
Book sales for North America and international:
Trafford Publishing, 6E–2333 Government St.,
Victoria, BC v8t 4p4 CANADA
phone 250 383 6864 (toll-free 1 888 232 4444)
fax 250 383 6804; email to orders@trafford.com
Book sales in Europe:
Trafford Publishing (uk) Ltd., Enterprise House, Wistaston Road Business Centre,
Wistaston Road, Crewe, Cheshire cw2 7rp UNITED KINGDOM
phone 01270 251 396 (local rate 0845 230 9601)
facsimile 01270 254 983; orders.uk@trafford.com
Order online at:
www.trafford.com/robots/04-1996.html

10 9 8 7 6 5 4

For Bryan Jr., Rebekah, David,
Nicole, Ashley, Rachel, and Naomi.

Acknowledgments

I would like to thank those who gave me feedback on various drafts of the book, particularly Arno Schmidt, who provided detailed notes on areas that needed clarification, Kate Holmes for her keen eye for grammar and punctuation, and my daughter, Nicole, whose careful proofreading and editing skills helped untangle some of my convoluted sentences and weed out some typographical errors I was blind to.

CONTENTS

Introduction

> Now for my life, it is a miracle of thirty yeares,
> which to relate, were not a History, but a peece
> of Poetry, and would sound to common eares
> like a fable.
>
> Sir Thomas Browne
> <u>Religio</u> <u>Medici</u>

This is not really an autobiography. Rather it is a series of autobiographical essays, sketches, meditations perhaps, focusing on persons or places that have a particular importance in my life. Each section was originally conceived of as a separate entity that could be read without regard to the other sections. However there are links between sections both in the way certain persons, places or incidents have formed transitions from one part of my life to another, and internally in the interlocking references to these persons or incidents which make connections in much the same way that the distinct curves and indentations of the pieces of a jigsaw puzzle hold the puzzle, as a whole, together.

I speak about "my life". But I think of it less as an ongoing story than as a series of "lives", some so distinct from the others one would almost think I had changed identities entirely. I see the early childhood section as being split into two very opposite parts--the happy time with my grandmother and the more disturbing time relating to my father and the convent. My growing up I associate primarily with the place--Palo Alto.

In my first marriage I stepped into a new and completely different world--a wide world of the Arts--both intellectually stimulating and wildly flamboyant. Because the person I married was older and his friends older still, their milieu was really that of the twenties through the forties. Their writers were Hemingway, F. Scott Fitzgerald, and William Faulkner, and like their icons, their drug of choice was alcohol.

My next incarnation (while simultaneously raising three children, getting a graduate degree and finally teaching) was as part of the psychedelic revolution in California. The person with whom I was primarily involved during that period, was my age, though he seemed much younger because I had been associating with people so much older. Moving to Carmel Highlands in the mid-sixties put me in the midst of all the experimentation and exploration that was part of the sixties revolution.

The influences of the sixties, primarily the taste for adventure, for seeking out exciting new experiences was what led me to Europe in 1967. That European period with its emphasis on French and Italian language and culture has, because of being married for fifteen years to the young student I met in Italy that year, remained with me in many ways up to the present. Even though I lived first in California and now in Canada and have been divorced for many years, I suppose as long as I retain the Garbarino name, I will always feel connected with the European part of my story.

Finally, however, I have reached a plateau in my life, free of either the emotional entanglements of relationships or the stressful concentration on trying to earn a living, a plateau from which I can look back and observe the wonderful, mysterious patterns of the "peece of poetry" that I call my life.

I suppose the other thing I want to make clear is that I make no claim for what I have written being "objective" or "factual", whatever those words mean. Ani de Franco, the singer and songwriter, has said that in poetry one must ignore the facts and focus on the truth. I have tried to do that in these essays. I make no claim to speak for anyone else but myself, and I fully recognize that what is truth for me can not and will not be truth for someone else. What I remember quite clearly of a particular incident is first of all filtered through the necessary selection filters of my unique background and previous experiences and then altered again by what my memory selects as the important details. What I have written is therefore, of necessity, "my reality", no one else's.

Chapter I

Grandmother Kirksey

It struck me, not so much on the first trip in 1960, stopping in Cannes, Nice, and Paris before heading off to London for a stint at the university, but certainly on the second visit in 1967, the inescapable feeling of somehow belonging in France. It was strange because as far as I knew I had no French ancestors. As a child I had memorized as a sort of catechism: "I am English, Irish, Scottish, Dutch, Swedish, and German", a recitation, which caused much amusement to the English family I was having dinner with shortly after my arrival on the first visit. How could I, a native Californian with both parents and grandparents born in the U.S., consider myself anything but American!

It wasn't until several years later that I discovered my French connection from a book my mother reluctantly passed on to me (she didn't appreciate the way she was described in the book)--a book by my maternal grandmother's cousin, a rambling, romanticized history of the Guyer family based on her own genealogical research and letters from various family members.

The German part was probably false, brought about by the fact that my ancestors, Huguenots fleeing southern France after the revocation of the Edict of Nantes, went first to Switzerland, apparently around Zurich which was then under German control, before migrating to Holland, and from there to the New World. Perhaps even the Dutch part was wrong, unless, of course, someone got married there before they set sail.

According to the book, the original French spelling of Guyer, my grandmother's maiden name, was "Guyere". The book traced the movement of our particular branch of the family from Pennsylvania, where Johan Henry Guyer landed when he arrived from Rotterdam in 1727, through Virginia, the Carolinas and Kentucky to Sedalia, Missouri, where my grandmother, Myra Jane Guyer, was born in 1868.

The book describes my grandmother's parents as landowners and slave owners who raised Arabian horses and my great grandmother, Amanda Florilla Marshall, as an "exceptional beauty with a strong character". She was said to have been the descendent of John Marshall, first chief justice of the U.S. Supreme Court, and a dedicated southerner who never forgave the "damned Yankees" for freeing their slaves, taking their horses, and then as the final insult making her cook the last of their chickens to feed the Yankee soldiers.

My grandmother's stories, as told to me as a child, began where the book leaves off. According to her, the family was poor when she was young. She never explained that it was the result of her family being on the wrong side in the civil war. She told stories of going barefoot much of the time and how the bramble and thistles hurt her feet. She said that going barefoot so much and then not having the proper size shoes when she did wear them was what caused her so much trouble with corns and bunions later on. It was ten miles to the nearest school and she had to ride bareback to get there.

When she was eighteen she moved to town and boarded with a minister and his wife to attend secretarial school. The minister's family had a buggy, which she said was a great treat--getting to ride to church in the buggy instead of having to walk or ride bareback.

Later she worked for a young doctor in town who, as she told it, had some romantic inclinations toward her. He would sometimes offer her a ride home from church in his buggy and one time made some excuse to take her hand. She told him that if he thought she was that sort of girl, he would just have to find someone else to do his shorthand for him. Apparently that rebuke was sufficient because he was a perfect gentleman after that--according to Grandmother partly because he feared losing a good secretary. The minister always used to say that Myra Jane was the one person he knew that God didn't need to keep much of an eye on because He could just trust her to do the right thing.

There were other potential beaus, but according to her, she didn't pay them much attention. It wasn't until the family moved to Texas and she met my grandfather that she found someone she was really interested in. I remember her saying, "As soon as I met your grandfather, all other men might as well have been stones in the road."

She did have one other beau of a sort, Wilford I think his name was. I know he wrote her several letters, one of which she got after she was married, not really love letters, you understand, but just the same she was so embarrassed that she handed the letter to my grandfather and then promptly forgot about the matter.

Weeks later, when my grandfather asked if she had answered the letter, she replied that she hadn't because she considered it improper for a married woman to correspond with a single gentleman--to which my grandfather gallantly replied that any young man who would write such a nice letter definitely deserved an answer.

I don't remember ever seeing a picture of my grandmother taken before she and Granddaddy were married. However I do remember one picture apparently taken several years after their marriage. It showed a relatively tall, solidly built woman with regular features and a cloud of soft brown hair piled on her head. As I remember the only incongruous feature in the photograph was a pair of metal-rimmed spectacles she was wearing. They seemed harsh in contrast to the soft swirl of curly hair and ample bosom.

In a child's developing consciousness whatever environment one finds oneself in seems natural and inevitable. One only realizes much later, after experiencing other families and other situations, that things might have been different. So my earliest memories of my grandmother and grandfather and the place where they lived didn't seem unusual.

I didn't find it strange, for example, that I lived with grandparents and didn't know who or where my parents were. I didn't think their large white house with its expansive lawn and its setting on a winding, palm tree-lined street different from anyone else's until one time when I was being dropped off after a birthday party and I observed the wide-eyed silence of the other children when the car stopped in front of the Kirksey house.

My earliest memories of my grandparents' place have a wonderfully warm, rich, dream-like quality to them. I remember the sensual smells of earth and flowers as I squatted in the flower beds at the side of the house to pick a bouquet of baby pink roses and blue forget-me-nots for Grandmother, the hissing sound and warm smells of water from the sprinklers hitting the hot pavement, and the insistent cooing of doves that gathered in the trees across the street where the city ended and the wilderness of Los Angeles canyons began. I can still feel the comfortable privacy of sitting in the lower branches of the tall cedar trees at the side of the house and smell the heady odors of the blossoms in the back yard magnolia tree where, if I climbed high enough, I could see the tiled swimming pool in the neighbor's yard.

Even on the rare occasions that Grandmother threatened to switch my legs for not finishing something on my plate, I don't remember feeling anything but absolute sureness that I was loved and protected and just where I should be. Perhaps I never actually got switched and knew it was an idle threat or perhaps

I felt so sure of Grandmother's love that whatever she did, I knew it would be the right thing for me.

One time, when I must have been very small because I was still sleeping in a crib beside her bed, I was frightened because I was sure there was a big glowing pumpkin under the crib that was going to "get me". Grandmother told me to jump out quickly and come into her bed. I ran as quickly as I could, and she held me, my head resting on her chest so I could feel her warmth and soothing heartbeat.

All my earliest memories of living first with my grandparents and later with just my grandmother have that kind of warm, comforting quality to them. Even though Grandfather Kirksey must have died when I was no more than four, I remember quite clearly walking hand in hand with him down the steep hill to Patterson's Drug Store on Colorado Boulevard, having a chocolate milkshake, and then stopping on our walk home to visit one of his friends who had a woodworking shop in his garage where he made furniture and boxes by assembling tiny pieces of wood into intricate patterns.

It occurred to me the other day in the middle of my usual afternoon slump, when I was craving something sweet and cold and creamy and was trying to talk myself into being satisfied with a piece of fruit instead, that perhaps what I really craved could be traced back to all that was associated with the time and place and circumstance of those chocolate milkshakes at Patterson's Drug store.

I remember the Kirksey house down to the smallest detail: the display case in the living room with the cups and trophies my uncles had won in track and field events and swimming, the objects on the shelf that included a photograph of some cotton fields and an actual ball of cotton still in its husk (a souvenir, I think, of the Kirksey side of the family), the oil painting over the fireplace of a southern-looking garden with weeping willow trees that I understood Grandmother Kirksey had painted. I even still remember the number of the phone that hung on the wall of the phone room that also served for hanging coats: ALBANY 4721.

The living room was large enough to have a parlor grand piano at one end and the usual living room furniture at the other-- couch, overstuffed chair, bookcase, and a rocker next to a table that held a dome-shaped radio. Between the two ends of the room was a large expanse of Oriental carpet that was my space for dancing to music from the wind-up Victrola at the piano's end of the room.

I loved to play the piano, mostly making up combinations of sounds that appealed to me, though I also was given some piano lessons at the time, along with ballet and drama lessons. My piano teacher was Mrs. Brosch who lived just up the street and was a friend of Grandmother's. Her house was on the canyon side of the street, hidden from view by trees and shrubs and reached by climbing up moss-covered flagstone steps under an arched entranceway.

The Kirksey house, though fairly impressive from the outside with its windows and doorways outlined with carefully trellised Jasmine, was fairly simple in design. After all, I think it was my grandfather who designed it and oversaw the construction, and he was an insurance executive, not an architect. It was basically a large box with rooms circling around a central core that contained the stairwells down to the basement or up to the top floor where the central hallway opened onto five bedrooms and a bath.

When I was very young, Grandmother's bedroom was at one end, and Granddaddy's was at the other. His room had a high dresser that, along with the eyeglasses and eye cups and sometimes a gold pocket watch, usually contained a Mounds bar that I was given a carefully cut one-inch piece of on special occasions. Another bedroom was designated for two of the "boys", my uncles, who must have been at least in their late thirties by then.

For awhile, the upstairs bedroom that had been Grandmother's when I was very little became a quilting room, filled almost completely with the large frame that Grandmother used for assembling hand-sewn quilts and where I first learned to use a needle and thread to put together scraps of quilting material to make dresses for my dolls.

Later, after Granddaddy had died and Grandmother's rheumatism no longer allowed her to climb stairs, the rooms upstairs were rented out to various tenants like the lady who was a devout Christian Scientist and read to me regularly from the Christian Science Monitor.

Grandmother moved into the dining room using a heavy folding bed with a mirrored front to sleep in at night and a commode instead of a toilet (since the only bathroom was upstairs). Her bathing thereafter was done, part by part, in the kitchen sink, and the commode was emptied each morning somewhere in the back yard to fertilize the dozen or so orange, lemon, and grapefruit trees that provided fresh fruit for breakfast or for lemonade on hot summer afternoons.

The scraps from the kitchen went to feed the chickens in a coop by the side fence, chickens that appeared from time to time on the dining room table roasted and ready to eat, though I never made the connection between the rust-colored, feathered strutters in the coop and the food on the table.

I don't know the details, but it seems that when Granddaddy died, despite having been in the insurance business, he had no life insurance. Grandmother, therefore, was left to cope pretty much on her own. Having lived most of her adult years with every available comfort, she found herself once again resorting to the ingenuity and thriftiness she had learned as a child. Once she moved into the dining room, all five bedrooms upstairs were rented out as well as the former sunroom, adjacent to the living room, and also the cottage in back, originally part of a double garage. Grandmother maintained her frugal ways from my childhood until she died when I was twenty, doing her own shopping even though it meant a tedious climb up the hill from the store on Colorado Boulevard, doing her own gardening, growing her own vegetables, raising chickens, and even climbing a ladder to paint the exterior of the house.

The only thing she ever complained about was her rheumatism. Other than that, her attitude was stolidly optimistic and purposeful. She went to church, took me to Sunday school, and was careful to teach me to say the Our Father and the Twenty-third Psalm. But I always felt that her faith came more from her own inner strength than from her Southern Methodist background.

The summer before she died I stayed with her for a while, as I had most summers after I moved to Palo Alto at the age of six to live with my mother. I was in my second year of college and was studying Roman Catholicism at the time, having been exposed to it by a friend a few years before. As I recall, Grandmother and I spent most of my time there discussing the philosophical implications of the Catholic doctrines in my catechism lessons. I remember thinking that, for an eighty-five-year-old woman from a conservative Protestant background, she was remarkably open minded.

It's not enough to say that Grandmother Kirksey was a special person for me, true though that is. The older I get, the more I wish I could go back and talk to her once again. There is so much more I would like to know. But this feeling is more than just nostalgia for my grandmother. I wish I could talk to her mother, Amanda Florilla, too. And I wonder what those years were like when their grandparents and great grandparents were moving across a gradually opening territory in the New World.

But I strongly feel my connectedness reaching farther back than that. I have walked the hills near tiny villages in southern France and visited the local churches and their adjoining graveyards and felt the sense that somewhere in that soil, somewhere among those ancient stones, the spirits of my ancestors still live. If I had spent more time in Ireland or Scotland or parts of England, I would probably feel the same sort of ancestral connection there too.

It would be wonderful, just once, to be a time traveler, to find myself at a village fair in Provence or Languedoc, let's say in the twelfth century, dancing to the music of the local piper and drummer, turning and whirling, hair and ribbons flying until, at the end of the dance, I would sink exhausted onto a hilly bank. Surely something in my blood knows what it was like to be there.

Chapter II

My Father

My father was a cowboy.

Well, not really, not quite. Though he did play cowboy "bit" parts in Hollywood movies back in the twenties--at least that's what somebody told me years ago, I don't even remember who. I never had any trouble believing it though. I can see it almost as clearly as if I had actually been there--his long, lanky frame astride a horse, cowboy hat tilted slightly to one side, left hand resting on the pommel of the saddle as he concentrated his attention on slowly and methodically rolling a cigarette with the other hand.

He was sort of a John Wayne, Gary Cooper type, tall and silent, and when he did speak, it was in a slow, laconic manner, almost a drawl. He was more of an urban cowboy though. Although he was often dressed in a fringed buckskin jacket and cowboy boots, the chequered shirts and tan gabardine pants he wore with them were always pressed and immaculate. Just as I never saw him ride a horse, I also never saw him dirty or dusty from the kind of labors a real cowboy would have been engaged in. One might have labeled him a "western aficionado" rather than a real cowboy.

When I was about ten and used to visit during summers, he was a deputy sheriff for Los Angeles County. It wasn't a full time job. He went to a meeting one night a week dressed in his uniform, with a gun and holster. He also had handcuffs I remember his putting on me just for fun and that I could always get out of easily. He probably would have enjoyed being in the military but didn't get the chance because of being too young for the first world war and too old for the second.

But if he was part cowboy, he was also part Indian. His main interest, aside from his work, which ranged from trucking to aeronautics to owning a sport shop, was working in silver and leather. He made intricate hand-tooled belts and handbags, even the twin buckskin jackets he and my stepmother, Rose, wore. And his silver and turquoise rings and bracelets would fool anyone but an expert into thinking they were genuine Navajo.

I'm sure that of all his jobs, the period of time when he owned the sport shop, a time stretching from my elementary school years until I was out of college, was his favorite. The store gave him a chance to sell items he enjoyed working with himself. In addition to the guns and other western items, he also sold ski apparel, tennis and badminton equipment, and archery bows, arrows and targets, some of which he brought home so he and Rose and my two half-brothers could practice every evening after dinner.

Despite his western orientation, however, he had never actually lived in the wild west or even on a ranch. He had been born in Pennsylvania and, when he was a child, went with his family to Panama where his father worked as an engineer on the Panama Canal. Sometime later, their family moved to Los Angeles, where he went through high school and eventually met my mother. The few years he spent living in Arizona running a trucking company with his brother during the depression (around the time I was born) were his closest experience to living in the real "west".

My earliest memory of my father was when I was in the convent. My mother had left me with her parents when she divorced my father and moved away to Palo Alto. But sometime during that period, from when I was about eighteen months old to six years old when my mother finally retrieved me, I ended up in a convent. I can only assume that the convent was my father's choice, since his family was Roman Catholic.

Perhaps I was taken away from Grandmother when Granddaddy Kirksey died, the Watkins side of the family assuming that Grandmother Kirksey was too distraught to care for me. I may have been in the convent for as long as six months, or perhaps two separate times. Eventually I was taken back to Grandmother Kirksey as I was losing weight and not in good health. You might think that if, at some point, Grandmother Kirksey couldn't care for me, the Watkins grandparents might have taken over, since the two families lived only a few miles apart. There are some clues in my memories of them to suggest why that didn't happen.

Grandfather Watkins was a heavy-set man who always seemed to be sitting in an overstuffed green leather chair smoking a pipe. Grandmother Watkins was small and frail, and rather than caring for me herself, always seemed to depend on my Aunt Ella to do things. It was Aunt Ella who scrubbed me in the bathtub with crocheted washcloths and Lifebuoy soap. It was Aunt Ella who made the beds with sheets so fresh off the line that I couldn't sleep for the intensity of their smell. I think Grandmother and Grandfather Watkins must have died when I was fairly young as those limited memories are all I have of them. I did have some souvenirs though--a white Catholic prayer book and a rosary that sat in my dresser drawer as I was growing up. I scribbled in the prayer book with crayons as a child, not knowing what else to do with it and thought for years the rosary was some kind of necklace. I also had, and still have, a small locket, not the kind that snaps open, but a green, enameled gold-edged leaf that slides open to reveal a miniature scene, with the word "Panama" printed underneath.

When I think of the convent, I see way high up on a shelf above me pale pastel Easter eggs and candies. I can't reach them and they are never taken down. They are wrapped in cellophane, but I can smell them just the same. There are other smells too, the liquid soap of the washrooms and the soup smell from the kitchen--even now the smell of public washrooms and cafeterias can bring a sort of hard, empty feeling to the pit of my stomach.

I remember certain incidents that happened in the convent too, like being left in my crib one day when all the other children had been taken out to play. It was a large high-ceilinged room with full-length windows along one wall and there were many cribs side by side. I wondered where all the other children were and why I had been left alone. Another memory is of one day being out on the playground and finding that one of my teeth had come out and that I had blood in my mouth. I was frightened because I didn't know teeth were supposed to come out and I had no one to ask about it. Another day, when we were in the dining room, the nuns went away and left some of the older girls in charge. They showed us the laundry chute and told us it was the way to hell and if we didn't eat with our forks instead of our spoons, they would shove us down the chute.

There are some pictures in the old family album of my father visiting me at my grandmother Kirksey's house, but I have no memory of those visits. The first time I remember seeing him was at the convent. It seems to me I was told that my father was coming to visit and something about the way it was told made it seem important. I'm not sure I would have known what the word "father"--or maybe they said "daddy"-- meant. I think I was dressed up for the occasion.

I remember crossing a sunlit courtyard and entering a room. It was dark and cool in contrast to the sunny courtyard. It had chairs placed just the right distance apart for people to carry on formal conversations. I don't remember what was said. I don't think I even really remember my father's presence there. What I do remember is that, just before he left, he gave me a coin, a nickel or dime, I don't remember which. I was running across the courtyard to show it to one of the nuns when I slipped and fell. I skinned my knees on the gravel and the coin tumbled out of my hand.

One of the nuns came running, scooped me up and took me to wherever they kept the pink stuff to put on hurt knees. She wiped my eyes and cleaned the gravel out of my scraped knee. She thought I was crying because my knee hurt. I tried to tell her about the coin but she didn't understand. She said not to worry, she would buy me a candy bar the next time she went into town to make up for the coin I had lost. I had no way to explain that what I had lost was not the monetary value of the coin but something that was of value because my father had given it to me and because that was all I had of him. Even if she had gotten me a candy bar, it would not have made up for what I lost that day. But even the candy bar was forgotten. I don't remember hearing any more about it.

Later, after my mother took me to live with her in Palo Alto, there were summer vacations I spent with my father and stepmother, even one school year (seventh grade) when I lived with them because my mother was getting a divorce from her second husband (there were three more to come). For me, the contrast between being with my mother and being at my father's house could hardly have been greater. My mother lived in a simple two-bedroom bungalow in one of the older residential areas of Palo Alto. She worked, mostly on electronics assembly lines, and after work spent her time in the bars in "Whiskey Gulch", the area on the other side of the Bayshore freeway where alcohol could be sold as it was illegal to sell it within the city limits of Palo Alto. She wasn't usually home for dinner, so I had to make do with whatever I could find in the house.

My father and stepmother's home, in contrast to my mother's, was always immaculate and they ran the house like they ran their lives--with a Germanic precision. There was a "right" way to do everything from dishes to dusting and vacuuming, ironing clothes and folding diapers (all of which I did a lot of after my two half-brothers were born). The attitude of my father and Rose seemed to be that I was a hopeless slob they needed to train extensively to save me from, in my father's words, turning out "just like your mother."

Never mind the fact that I was genetically inclined from the start to be more like my father than my mother and that when I was living at my mother's house, my room was always neat, my clothes always cleaned and pressed, and if the rest of the house got cleaned at all, I was the one who did it.

Those visits to my father's house and the year in seventh grade that I lived with them were extremely painful. I don't remember ever hearing a single kind, encouraging word from my father. I had already been told more than once by my mother that she cried when I was born because, although she had wanted a girl, my father was hoping for a boy. Now he had his boys--two of them, in fact--and he didn't need me. I knew instinctively that my visits must be embarrassing for my father, evidence of his previous failed marriage, something that didn't fit with the image of the perfect all-American family he seemed to be trying to project.

He seldom spoke to me directly. Most of what he had to say was filtered through Rose often in the form of "we think..." or we have decided that..." I should not be allowed more than one soft drink per day or I should not wear lipstick.

Most embarrassing was the time we had been invited to go swimming at the house of some friends of theirs. I was having a good time racing around the pool with the other children--I was in early adolescence at the time. Rose drew me aside and whispered to me that my father said to tell me that I should do something about the fact that I had hair showing at the bottom of my bathing suit. What could I do? I didn't know of anything to do but to feel humiliated.

At some point toward the end of the year I spent with them, Rose asked me to go into the living room because my father wanted to talk to me. Again, as in the convent, we were seated across from each other in a formal interview. I wondered what was wrong this time. My father started by listing all of the things he and Rose had done for me, presumably to rescue me from turning out "just like your mother". He said that after much thought he and Rose had decided that I should stay with them instead of going back to Palo Alto to live with my mother. I don't remember his exact words but they certainly did not include the concept of "love". My impression was that they were offering to make a great sacrifice on their part because it was their "duty" to see that I was taken care of and obviously my mother was not competent to do it.

I don't remember if I gave him my answer immediately but I do know what I thought. I couldn't wait to get out of that room, out of that house and back to Palo Alto. It wasn't my mother that I was anxious to get back to. How could I explain that being more or less on my own in a non-judgmental environment was far better than being the perpetual outsider in their perfect world?

Even when it came to presents there was always discomfort. I dreaded opening their Christmas gifts when they were delivered to my mother's house. They were items I knew had come from the shelves of my father's sporting goods store-

-things I wouldn't be caught dead in and that I knew I would have to lie about when I wrote them a "thank-you" letter. Later, when I was older and in high school, they sent me handbags that looked like the kind old ladies carried. What was I supposed to do with them?

The only exception to the problem of presents came one year when I was allowed to choose what I wanted from the sport shop. I had just taken up skiing and chose ski pants and a parka that was actually the only ski outfit I ever owned. I think for the next gift occasion I got to choose a belt and some goggles to go with my outfit.

I also remember the gift my mother sent me for Christmas the year I was staying with my father. It was a large, round, ornate container of "Shanghai" perfume. My father and Rose were horrified at anyone sending such an inappropriate gift to a twelve-year-old girl. I was in seventh heaven!

When I moved away from my mother's house in Palo Alto to live in a boarding house in San Jose at the beginning of my second year of college, my mother and I made an agreement that she would pass on to me the $70 per month my father was sending her for child support. Other than that, I was to be completely on my own, earning what I could part-time during the school year and full time during the summer. I had no doubt

I could survive as I had started working part time at fifteen and by that time had worked several summers as a swimming instructor and lifeguard in addition to the various part-time jobs as sales clerk and cashier. I managed fairly well except for a few weekends at the boarding house when I ran out of money for food.

A problem arose, however, in my last year of college. I was turning twenty-one in October and my father was only required to pay child support until that birthday. I wrote to him asking if he would extend the $70 a month payments until June when, presumably, I would graduate. He wrote back saying he couldn't afford the extra expense--despite the fact that he and Rose had moved a few years before into a spacious, ranch-style home in an up-scale part of Glendale. He also said, though I'm sure I had heard him say it before, that he didn't see any reason for girls to go to college as they were just going to get married anyway.

Well, I can't deny he was right in a way about that. I managed to get through the school year somehow and only needed to do my term of student teaching in the fall to finish my B.A. in General Elementary Education. But shortly after school was out in June, I married an eccentric and fascinating artist I had met just two months earlier.

Bryan was hardly the sort of person I expected my father and Rose to approve of. He and my mother got along fine--they were both alcoholics, so when my mother wanted a drink there was always a good supply around. Oddly enough, when Bryan and I drove down to Glendale a short time after we were married so he could meet my father and Rose--they weren't at the wedding--my father seemed quite pleased with Bryan. I even remember him saying something to Bryan about how, now that I was married, I would have someone to look after me. Funny, because I knew even then that it was I who was going to be doing the "looking after", not Bryan.

When Bryan and I divorced some five years and three children later, I knew that in my father's eyes I had failed again--never mind Bryan's drinking and psychological problems and my lack of preparedness for having three children in less than four years. So I simply got lost--that is I changed addresses and didn't let my father and Rose know where I had moved to. I went back to work and then back to school taking four years to complete my B.A. and then M.A. in English, all the while in the back of my mind thinking that what I was doing would prove something to my father about my worth as a person.

After I finished my degrees, I taught for one year at San Jose State College where I had done my undergraduate work. I had been seeing Mel since Bryan and I separated, and Mel and I were married during the Christmas break that year, In June, as soon as the school term was over, I moved to Carmel, where Mel was working.

It was time to try again to contact my father. After all, Mel was the kind of steady, reliable person my father might relate to. Besides I had accomplished something by getting my degrees and landing a good teaching job--I was ignoring the remarks my father had made about girls going to college. So I wrote and got a letter back saying that Dick, the youngest of my half-brothers, was getting married and inviting me down for the wedding. This seemed like the perfect opportunity to get to know my brothers who had been too young to relate to the last time I had been at my father's house. I took my youngest son, David, and made the trip to Glendale.

I had thought I was prepared, that my ego was sufficiently secure to be able to exude healthy self-confidence in the presence of my father's family. I was wrong. I felt the cloud of self-doubt descending as soon as I passed the Los Angeles city limits, and by the time I arrived at my father's house, whatever bravado I managed to show on the outside was a thin veneer over an insecure seventh-grade adolescent.

Fortunately, the family was too busy with preparations for the wedding to pay much attention to me. I had made arrangements to stay in another part of L.A. with a friend of mine who had recently moved from San Francisco. So, aside from a family dinner at the bride-to-be's house and the wedding itself, there was minimal contact with the family. I did make an effort to communicate with Bill, the older of my brothers, by asking him to join my friend and me for dinner. He declined, possibly for some good reason, but given my state of mind I assumed it could only be because my brothers had absorbed the negative family attitude toward me and were not interested in getting to know me better.

That conclusion, however hasty at the time, seemed to be confirmed by something that happened several months later. I was back in Carmel, living in a large Spanish-style house in Carmel Highlands, when I got a call one afternoon from Marianne, Dick's new bride. It seems he had been drafted into the army and was stationed at Fort Ord, just outside of Monterey. She had come up to visit him and needed a place to stay. I told her we had plenty of room.

She arrived sometime after supper and, since Mel was out of town and the children with their father, Marianne and I had time to sit in the kitchen that evening and talk. I told her a lot of things about my experiences with the family and how I felt about them.

Eventually we went off to bed, she in the children's bedroom upstairs and I in the master bedroom. When I got up in the morning she was gone, no note, no good-bye, nor did I ever hear from her or Dick again. Did I tell her too much--things that she found uncomfortable to hear? I guess I'll never know.

By the time I contacted the family again, twenty years had passed. I had gotten "lost" once again, this time by going off to Europe and spending much of the next two years there. Mel was agreeable, as usual. He said I could come back any time I wanted to, but by now I knew that meant a sort of open marriage arrangement in which he agreed to pay the bills as long as I didn't ask too many questions about what he was doing with his time. And I knew that whatever ideas I had about marriage or relationships, that was not what I wanted.

When I finally wrote to Rose from Vancouver in 1984, it was because I felt an urge to thank her. From a more mature perspective, I knew that she had not been in an enviable position trying to bridge the gap between me and my father and that, although she had seemed like the stereotypical mean stepmother at the time, she had really tried to do what she thought was best for me.

I was addressing the letter to her because instinctively I knew that my father was dead. I was right. When I talked to her on the phone she confirmed that he had died a few years before. What I was not prepared to hear was that Dick had died of leukemia in his mid-thirties and Bill, the older brother, had been married and divorced and had had a son who died of cancer before his second birthday. It was something of a revelation to me to discover that this perfect family could experience ordinary human misfortunes.

But family myths die hard. One of the first things Rose said to me when I got her on the phone was, "You aren't in any trouble are you?" I almost laughed. Who me? The one all my friends knew as a perfectionist and control freak. The one who took charge of committees, who was always reliable and punctual, whose house was always organized and immaculate, down to the folded socks and underwear in the drawers.

The other thing I remember her saying, somewhere about the middle of our conversation, was that my father had been very hurt when I didn't try to contact them again after I had been down for the wedding. She said they had tried phoning Mel and been told I had gone off to Europe. My first reaction was that, being the loyal wife she was to my father, she would have to think his feelings were hurt because he cared about me. I was sure she was only inventing a fiction that suited her idealized image of the man she had married.

But then a friend pointed out to me that, after all, she had lived with my father for more than fifty years. Who could have known him better than she did? What if there were even a little bit of truth to what she said? What did I really know about the man I called my father, the strong but silent urban cowboy from whom I inherited a certain shyness and reticence, an often distant attitude toward other people. How can I know, on the basis of selective memory, what is truth and what is fiction?

Chapter III

Palo Alto

The Kirksey family was part of the Palo Alto community when the town was still in its infancy, merely an adjunct to recently established Stanford University. My mother grew up in a large Victorian home on Cowper Street that the family occupied while she attended high school and her older brothers made their mark as track and field stars at Stanford.

There must have been some socializing between the family and the university founders as my mother's mention of certain people the family had known elicited awe from those old enough to know who was who in the early social structure of the university.

I suppose she proved those connections by landing me my first job at fifteen as cashier in a restaurant and homemade candy store owned by one of the early Stanford group. These social connections plus my mother's fond memories of growing up in Palo Alto make it easy to understand why she chose to return there after she and my father separated. And, as it turned out, Palo Alto was a good place for me to grow up too.

The house Grandfather Kirksey had bought for my mother (and homesteaded so she couldn't lose it for non-payment of taxes) was a simple two-bedroom bungalow. It sat on a Maple tree-lined street behind an L-shaped block containing every conceivable amenity. At one end of this five-block-long property was a rambling, Spanish-style community center that had adult and children's theaters as well as Boy Scouts and Cubs and, in the basement, a space turned over to the pre-teens as a "rec center". The large expanse of lawn in front became a forest of pastel ribbon bedecked maypoles every May Day.

Directly behind the community center, connected to it by a walled-in "Secret Garden" only opened on special occasions, was the children's library, the frequent setting for presentations by children's authors and illustrators. I loved the murals that illustrators of children's books had painted on the walls and the storytelling visits by authors, but I don't remember being a regular library visitor. The children's books that were classics for children or the ones that won the Caldecot Award each year neither reflected the realities of my childhood nor gave me the sort of escapes my imagination craved.

My two favorite books--the only books I owned and which I read over and over again--were Hawthorne's *Tanglewood Tales,* a retelling of the Greek myths, and Mark Twain's *The*

Prince and the Pauper. My other favorite reading material, I must confess, was comic books, not the typical Disney type, which I disdained as much as the usual popular books for children. My tastes ran to exotic adventure tales, preferably with strong women as the central character, my favorite being *Sheena, Queen of the Jungle.*

Across the parking lot from the community center and library were the Girl Scout house and the Junior Museum with its collection of odd snakes and other scaly creatures and an extra room that served for children's clay modeling classes. After a stretch of open playing fields, Walter Hays Elementary school opened onto Middlefield Road and, opening onto the back street nearer my house, there was a playground and a series of tennis courts. Near the end of the block, double swimming pools fronted onto a small park and picnic area and, just behind the pools, was the dense grove of evergreens which we all referred to as the "Magic Forest" and which I passed through nearly every day in the summer to reach the pool entrance

Having sources of activities so close meant that I hardly minded the lack of a family atmosphere at home. I wasn't extrovert enough to participate in the children's plays, but loved to hang around the dressing rooms and see all the fairytale costumes being constructed. I joined the Girl Scouts and took classes in pottery and clay modeling at the Junior Museum and attended Walter Hays Elementary.

But most of my time was spent at the playgrounds or at the swimming pool. I have seen some notes I wrote as a child that read, "Dear Mother, I hav gon to the polygrons". There must have been many of those notes as that was where I went most afternoons after school when my mother was still at work. I knew it was time to come home when the five o'clock whistle blew.

Those early years from first to sixth grade when my mother was married to her second husband were, for the most part, ordinary and pleasantly uneventful. My stepfather was an easygoing man, a plumber by trade, who seemed to have a genuine affection for me. The affection was not demonstrated physically, possibly because he knew something about the potential dangers of stepfather/stepdaughter relationships that I did not. He had a gentle quixotic sense of humor that usually took the form of verbal put-ons. When I asked for his opinion about something, he would respond with a long somber pause followed by, "Well, when I was a Girl Scout". We also wrote love notes to one another in which I called him "daddy" and to which he responded with deliberately outrageously distorted spelling--at least I think it was deliberate.

The only unpleasant times were when he and my mother had friends over for a party because that meant lots of drinking and louder and louder talking as the evening wore on, making it almost impossible for me to sleep as my bedroom was only a door away from the front room where the party was taking place. The thing I dreaded most was that someone would decide to play the ukulele I had tucked away on my bedroom shelf and which I didn't want anyone to touch, especially a drunk. I usually lost the battle for possession and had to cringe in silence in my room hoping my treasure would survive their drunken molestation.

But all in all, it was a good time. My mother and stepfather never yelled at each other or at me. I wasn't criticized or given excessively stringent rules to abide by. I was generally left to do what I chose, when I chose, with whom I chose, and I did not abuse the privilege.

This period was the only time when my mother, in spite of working full time, really made an attempt to play the "mother" role. She cooked fairly regularly, even preparing the occasional Thanksgiving or Christmas meal complete with Velveeta cheese-stuffed stalks of celery and pimiento stuffed green olives. She even made some pretty good pies from the apples that hung over on our side of the fence from the neighbor's yard.

When I think of how to describe my mother, the phrase that keeps coming to mind is the title of a song, "Girls just want to have fun." She didn't mind working on electronics assembly lines as long as there were pleasant, easy-going people to work with. But mostly she enjoyed after work going to the bars in "Whiskey Gulch", where University Boulevard ended at Bayshore freeway.

I remember numerous phone calls from her around supper time, a cheery voice saying she had just run into "a friend of your uncle Frank's" and wouldn't be home for dinner and could I fix myself something. The trouble was there was usually nothing to fix, I had no money, and the nearest store or restaurant, even if I had had money, was at least four miles away. From ninth grade on, fortunately, there were boyfriends with cars to take me out for a hamburger at one of the drive-ins.

My mother was an attractive woman, not beautiful, but tall and slim with auburn hair done in the side-parted and waved fashion of the thirties. Her style was a simple tailored look, pant suits mostly with flat shoes, sort of the Joan Crawford type, only softer and prettier.

Because her father had sent her to a fancy girl's finishing school in the south, she had an aura of cultivation that seemed to impress people. She spoke well, never using slang or making grammar mistakes and had a gift for writing charming notes and letters. Her reading, however, was limited, consisting of the occasional popular novel or *Reader's Digest* and, in her later years, *The Enquirer* and other scandal sheets. There never were more than one or two books of hers in the house and of those I recall only an ancient copy of Longfellow's *Evangeline*.

Her two prized possessions were a diamond ring her father had given her and a fur coat, a Russian Squirrel I think it was, which probably came from her father too. Over the years the diamond got hocked again and again whenever she ran out of money and eventually disappeared. The coat was carefully put in storage each summer and restyled several times until finally it became quite scraggly. But my mother still wore it. I'm reminded of my daughter Bekah's security blanket that, by the time she was in her thirties, was nothing more than pieces of shredded nylon she still kept tucked under the covers at the foot of her bed. Come to think of it, that's probably just what that fur coat was--my mother's security blanket.

Her other prize possession, though there was disagreement about it, was the piano. It was the same parlor grand that had, when I lived with my maternal grandparents, graced one end of their enormous living room. Some time after we moved into the house in Palo Alto, the piano arrived. My grandmother said she was sending it to me so I could continue the piano lessons I had started when I was living with her in Eagle Rock. My mother said the piano was hers, that her father had given it to her. But since he was already dead by that time, there was no way to settle the argument. She could only play "Barcarole", and I only kept up my lessons for about six months, but the piano continued to take up nearly half the space in our small living room until I finally sold the house for demolition some forty years later.

My mother was a generally cheery, agreeable person, at least until the last few years. She didn't complain or nag or try to belittle people, though she did have what I found to be an annoying tendency to pry into other people's finances. She was generally pleased with whatever I did, though she also seemed to have no particular expectations. My grades were fine whatever they were. She didn't have any thoughts about my going to college and never mentioned the word "career". When I talked about getting married to my first serious boyfriend, she wasn't concerned but said I should finish high school first. I was told that she carried pictures of me around which regularly got shown to people she met in the bars.

Perhaps because she had been somewhat spoiled by her father and felt alienated from her mother, she felt more comfortable with men. She expected men to adore her and wait on her, even into her eighties, and mostly she got her way. Even my husbands couldn't resist her charming way of asking them to drop whatever they were doing to run to the store for a bottle of vodka.

She had very few women friends, but those she had she was quite loyal to. My father's sister, Aunt Ella, had been one, and there was another friend in Los Angeles named Beula that I heard a lot about over the years but don't remember meeting. The only woman friend I remember from Palo Alto was the mother of one of my friends. She was a young looking, if slightly overdone, blonde generally considered to be a nymphomaniac. She hung out in the same bars as my mother, but had the reputation of ending up in the back rooms with various men. She had five children, my friend being the oldest and, she bragged, the only one fathered by her husband. Various people tried to convince my mother not to hang around with Claire, insisting that my mother had too much "class" to associate with someone like that. But my mother didn't seem to care. A friend was a friend, and she truly enjoyed Claire's company, even her outrageous behavior.

By the time I reached my early teens I was treated less like a child than like another adult. My mother took me into bars with her on several occasions and wasn't even upset when the bartender made a mistake and put whiskey in the Coke I had ordered. There were times when I actually felt more as if I were the mother and she the daughter. In between marriages she would often ask my opinion about someone she was dating or have me answer the phone to ward off advances from an admirer she wasn't interested in.

When her fourth husband (the third had died of a heart attack only about a year after they were married) got angry at her one day and chased her around the house with a butcher knife, I was the one who calmed him down and took the knife away. Traumatic as it may sound, I don't remember feeling traumatized. It just seemed that something sensible had to be done, and since the adults in the house were behaving like children or worse, it was up to me to behave like an adult.

But for the most part during those years I was more concerned with my friends than with my family (or lack thereof). The first friend to make a lasting impression was Toy, a girl I had met in fourth grade. She was my first exposure to intellectual eccentricity.

Her parents were divorced and her mother, a nurse, worked nights at the hospital which gave us ample opportunity to roam the streets at night, even occasionally, on warm summer evenings, climbing over the fence at the pool for a midnight swim. My first introduction to literature was through Toy, who by junior high was keeping me awake most of the nights I was supposedly "sleeping over" by reciting Shakespeare or Byron, Shelley, and Keats. Not reading, mind you, but reciting from memory.

Not surprisingly, Toy was determined to be an actress, which indeed she was for a short time, after she had married and divorced her English professor at Cornell. We even had a plan for after we were out of high school (I hadn't considered how this plan conflicted with my plans to marry my boyfriend upon graduating). We were going to go to New York together, she to become a famous actress and I to become a top model. I even had my model name picked out--Mauri Stevens. I guess Toy thought her own name, Toy Storey, was exotic enough.

Our plans were foiled however when, in our senior year, Toy's mother discovered that my mother had taken us to San Quentin prison to visit the brother of one of our classmates who had been sent there as "an example" after a number of minor run-ins with the law. Toy was shipped off to her father on Long Island, and it was several years before we encountered one another again.

Then, of course, there were boyfriends. My first love, in eighth grade, was Don, a sort of James Dean type the same age as myself but one grade behind because he had flunked. At that stage our group was having parties at different houses one evening each weekend that consisted of turning down the lights, putting some records on, and dancing a slow two-step in time to the music. It was a great chance to get close to members of the opposite sex without much danger as all that ever happened beside dancing was the occasional kiss, the parents usually being somewhere in another part of the house and sticking their heads into the living room from time to time to make sure nothing was getting out of hand.

For me, who had had so little closeness with males, the effect was overwhelming. I became dizzy and lightheaded. The room seemed to glow with an ethereal light, and Don seemed transformed into the ultimately perfect essence of maleness. I was madly in love, a love which consisted of my seeing him on weekends, writing about him in my diary, and "going steady" (wearing his ring on a chain around my neck) for twenty-three whole days--until he decided he was more attracted to another girl in our group and asked for his ring back.

Since this was my first love, it took me awhile to get over it and, after all, in eighth grade I was still feeling awkward and ill at ease with boys. I even still had braces on my teeth. By the end of ninth grade, however, all that had changed. The braces were off and I had grown more comfortable with my five foot seven inch height. I began to be surprised by wolf whistles when walking past construction sites. It wasn't long before there were high school boys in their cut-down, souped-up cars cruising the route I took walking home from school. One of these boys turned out to be a very nice, if somewhat shy, high school junior named Paul, and within a few weeks I had a new "steady" boyfriend.

Paul and I "went" together on and off all through high school, though there were plenty of other boys to date in the "off" periods. Some of them were great dancers, and I loved to dance. One was a star on our high school football team whose school sweater I wore for awhile. Some were fraternity guys from Stanford, so I went to a lot of "frat" dances and parties. But I always went back to Paul, and Paul was always there to go back to. I was flattered by the attention I got from all the other boys, but it was Paul's dogged devotion that made me feel most at ease with him. I'm sure he remained a loyal and faithful husband to the girl he finally married, but by the time he returned from serving in the Navy in Korea, I had graduated, gone off to San Jose State College and was beginning to glimpse new horizons that I knew Paul would never share.

My time in Palo Alto ended after the first year at State. I had commuted the first year, but even so, the transition from high school to college had not been easy. My high school's population had been about five hundred. State's was twenty-five thousand. I began to have dizzy spells in the coffee shop in the morning before classes. I felt as if I were inside a huge glass dome that I could see out of and everyone else could see into, but that I couldn't really touch or contact anyone. I didn't realize until many years later, when I read Sylvia Plath's *The Bell Jar,* that anyone else might have had a similar experience. I dropped out the second quarter and spent the time finger-painting and talking to someone I had met while commuting that first term. By the time I went back in the spring term, I had a new and, to me, very important friend.

Fran wasn't one of the Palo Alto kids I had grown up with. He was a few years older, had just gotten out of the army, and was returning to college. He didn't seem to mind being called on at all hours to listen to my problems. Fran's demeanor was that of serenity and patience and, unlike most of my male contacts up to that point, he was interested in something other than football, cars, or parties.

More than that, he never took advantage of me sexually, which he might easily have done, considering my generally confused state. He was from a very Catholic background, his sister being a nun and brother a priest, but his approach to Catholicism was less the usual rote acceptance and more in the vein of Catholic scholars and philosophers. He was finishing his degree in English literature and, like Toy, his enthusiasm for ideas generally, particularly as expressed in literature and poetry, was stimulating in a way that not much in either my home environment or school experience had been.

Fran, like Toy, had touched a responsive chord, introducing me to a world that I didn't even quite yet know existed. My relationship with Fran persisted through my years at San Jose State even though by my third year he had moved away to complete a Master's degree. There was even a brief heady time in our correspondence when he proposed and I accepted though I was sure I could not possibly live up to either his expectations or those of his family.

My merely expressing those concerns, or perhaps his own good sense, seems to have brought him to the same conclusion because a short time later, he withdrew his proposal. But not before he had done two very important things for me-- supporting and encouraging me through the difficult transition from high school to college, from home (such as it was) to being entirely on my own, and introducing me to college courses and instructors that would serve as a springboard for changes about to come.

My relation to school up to and including my first years of college had been desultory at best. School was just someplace I went during the day because everyone else did. There was no pressure to get anything better than average grades, though I distinctly remember repeated high school teacher's comments on my report cards and during conferences that went something like, "Does not work to capacity".

I had no idea what they meant. What was my "capacity"? I remember taking numerous I.Q. tests in which I thoroughly enjoyed the complicated spatial and verbal puzzles I was given. But it was against school policy to give out the scores on those tests, so no one but my teachers and whoever scored the tests ever knew the results. No one ever said, "Here is a bright girl who should be encouraged to go to college". Only the ubiquitous "does not work to capacity" which had no meaning to me and apparently not to my mother either.

There had been the rare occasion in high school when an assignment caught my interest and I spent some time working on it. In my junior year, for example, we were reading *A Tale of Two Cities* and our assignment gave me the opportunity to create a piece of fiction based on that work. I spent days in the library, a rare occurrence for me, crafting the interior monologue of a prisoner waiting to be taken to the guillotine at dawn. When the teacher returned my paper, it had an "A" on it, but some remarks I didn't understand. Talking to him about the paper was the first time I had ever heard the word "plagiarism". Apparently he was so surprised that I was capable of that level of work that he thought I must have copied it.

College was not much different. My main focus, at least at first, was social rather than intellectual. I had to work part time, of course, but that didn't interfere with attending football games and frat parties on weekends. The only intellectually stimulating classes I remember in the first two years were English classes, in one of which we spent most of the time talking about Greece and the Greek myths. The other was a class in which I wrote another short story based on my father's visit to the convent. It wasn't until the third and fourth years, taking courses like Oriental Literature, Oriental Philosophy, and Existential Philosophy, some of which Fran had recommended, that my intellectual horizons began to broaden.

In the spring term of my fourth year at San Jose State, shortly after Fran had broken our brief engagement, a mutual friend of Fran's and mine insisted that I accompany him up into the Santa Cruz mountains to meet another friend of his, an artist, who was living on a "ranch" on Skyline Boulevard. It was actually 250 acres of pear and apple orchards with one of two barns converted into a studio.

After a short courtship, which included more displays of paintings, literary works and music than I had ever experienced in my life up to that point, Bryan proposed. He said we should get married, not because we were in love (we had spent much of our time discussing my love for Fran and his continuing love for his first wife) but because, as he put it, he was a really good painter but was going to drink himself to death if I didn't marry him and help straighten him out so he could continue his painting.

It was an offer I couldn't refuse. I had never met anyone even remotely like Bryan, not even Fran, and was pretty sure that I was unlikely to meet anyone like that again, so I said "yes" and we were married just after school was out in June, barely two months after we had met.

Chapter IV

Bryan

The nightingales are sobbing
In the orchards of our mothers
And hearts that we broke long ago
Have long been breaking others.

W.H. Auden

I had actually encountered Bryan Wilson several years before. My first job at fifteen had been cashiering and working behind the counter in a combination restaurant and candy store in Palo Alto. There was a soda fountain across from the candy counter and, further back, a series of high-backed booths finished, like the counters, in richly polished dark wood.

We had a range of customers, from sedate, middle-aged couples having dinner to teenagers dropping by for a soda. One category of patron, naturally, was Stanford students, since we were located on a corner just one block on the other side of the overpass from the Stanford campus. I was too young to pay much attention to them, though I do remember one night when a group of students sitting in a back booth got kicked out for filling glasses with varying amounts of water and making sounds by rubbing circles around the rims.

Bryan was with this group, perhaps along with his first wife--they had been married about that time when they were both just twenty-one. What I remembered later about Bryan was his stern looks, his arched nose, and what seemed to me then a strange combination of attire--low-slung jeans and a very expensive looking sports coat with patches on the sleeves.

*****

Bryan had entered Stanford at sixteen as the result of a California statewide exam given to identify students who might benefit from early admission to university and thereby avoid the draft. He and another student at his high school in Modesto placed first and second on the exam for the entire state. In spite of his obvious artistic talent, his mother had insisted on his registering in pre-med. That lasted until the end of his third year when he took off for Chicago where, he told me, he stayed for several months living in a basement room and eating nothing but doughnuts. It was probably his first time away from home and away from his mother's smothering attention.

He must have later come to some agreement with his parents because eventually he returned to Stanford, this time as an art major, taking up residence (illegally) with his friend, sculptor Oliver Andrews, in the attic of the old barn that was used as studio space by the art department. (It is now filled with trendy shops, a part of the Stanford Shopping Center).

But by the time my friend Thorne took me to meet this strange artist who lived on a ranch on the top of a mountain, I had long since forgotten most of what had taken place six years before at the restaurant.

In thinking back about it now, Bryan's two-month courtship reminds me most of the mating displays of Beauregard, the peacock on Bryan's ranch--the brilliant colors, the shimmering vibrations of the courting dance, the prancing back and forth in front of Jemimah and Jocasta, the two seemingly disinterested peahens. Bryan showed me his paintings and talked about his reasons for painting and his theories of painting. In fact, I was given a crash course on the whole history of painting, illustrated from the art books in Bryan's library.

He had extensive knowledge, not only about painting, but literature and music as well. He read aloud to me from W.H.

Auden, Dylan Thomas, Ezra Pound, and Wallace Stevens among others. He told personal anecdotes about authors that turned out to be useful later when I returned to college to finish my degree. Part of this was first-hand information as he had a habit of phoning well-known people when he had been drinking. He managed to get Ezra Pound on the phone while Pound was being held at St. Elizabeth's mental hospital in Washington and would have talked to Wallace Stevens but his timing was wrong--Wallace Stevens was dying at the time.

As background music to our candle-lit, wine-accompanied dinners held in the kitchen of the old farm house he had renovated in typical Bryan Wilson style, we listened to recordings of Bach partitas and sonatas performed by Wanda Landowska on what was perhaps the same harpsichord she had given to Bryan's Stanford acquaintance, Putnam Aldrich.

I remember Putnam and me trying to squeeze together into Bryan's Porsche after a concert at the Bach festival in Carmel. The question was whether the diminutive Putnam should sit on my lap or me on his. It was finally decided that it was more practical for him to sit on my lap than the reverse.

Bryan had met numerous, to me quite exotic, people during his stay at Stanford. There was the daughter of one of the original ranching families in California whose parents still owned thousands of acres. She had a weight problem she dealt with by going out to sea on her twelve-man crew, ocean-going yacht, presumably with a supply of diet foods. Another was son to the Dutch consul in Hawaii whose name, I remember, was Jan Englebert Rinehart Einhoven Von Twillhart Depauw.

Then there was Frederic Spiegelberg, Stanford philosophy professor, who taught a highly regarded, if somewhat controversial, comparative religions class in the basement of a church and specialized in Hindu philosophy and Tibetan ghost traps.

None of these people would have seemed out of place at Stanford, then or now. But for me, coming from my modest background and compared to the people I had encountered at San Jose State College, Bryan's friends were like something out of a novel.

Bryan himself was no less flamboyant. Just as his way of dressing might combine jeans with Harris Tweed sports coats, his renovations to the old farmhouse reflected his eclectic style. The kitchen had been painted by a drunken party of his friends one night. Each section of the old panel walls had been colored a different brilliant hue with seemingly no concern for what color the person painting the adjoining panel might have used.

The adjacent living room was just the opposite. Bryan had turned one wall into a dark wood bookcase and fitted an Empire-style couch covered in moss green fabric into the space next to the stone fireplace. The only other furniture in the room was a dark green leather chair and matching footstool and a large round table in a style matching the couch upon which sat a lamp made from a glass flask over two feet in diameter. Oh yes, and then there was the albatross.

In addition to his paintings, Bryan had done a number of wood sculptures of birds. Several of these were displayed on the unfinished plywood table in the third room downstairs, originally a dining area, that Bryan was using as a gallery. The albatross was the largest of his wood sculptures, life size actually, with a wingspan of over six feet. Bryan had hung it above the living room fireplace.

One evening some neighbors from several miles down Skyline Boulevard were there for dinner. As we were having after-dinner drinks in the living room, the man, who was sitting next to the fireplace, suddenly turned pale and passed out. We managed to get a doctor from somewhere, God knows where as the nearest town was at least thirty minutes away over very steep and winding, partly unpaved roads. At any rate, the doctor examining our friend stretched out on the floor asked him to look up intending to say "at the ceiling". But when he looked up himself, paused for a moment, and then as if it were the most normal thing in the world to have a six-foot albatross hanging from one's ceiling, said calmly "at the albatross."

Agnes was also part of the living room decor. I don't know why Bryan started calling her Agnes, though I now think of her as "Agnus Dei." Agnes is a four-foot high marble Kuan Yin bodhisattva. Bryan had seen her at Gumps in San Francisco several years before we were married. Her price tag said "$150", and Bryan thought that was a remarkably good price. So, not having any money with him, he charged Agnes to his Gumps account. The problem was that someone had made a mistake. The price was supposed to be $1500. Bryan got a call from Gumps asking him to please allow them to change the amount of the charge. But in typical Bryan fashion, he refused, and Agnes the cut-rate bodhisattva has been in the family ever since. Having had her head knocked off twice by rambunctious children, she now sits serenely near the fireplace in my Vancouver condo.

*****

During the weeks leading up to and during our wedding, my strongest feeling was that of being a sacrificial lamb led to the slaughter. Which is strange because no one was leading me except myself. I knew my feelings were not the kind of romantic idealized attachment I had expected to feel (that girls generally expected to feel during the late forties and early fifties when they got married). But some part of me was saying I had stumbled across an opportunity--a chance to open doors to a new, creative, intellectually stimulating life that was rare and special, one I would never become involved in if I didn't take the chance that was being offered to me at that moment.

To someone else it might have seemed an opportunity of a different sort. Bryan's parents were well off financially and his mother, particularly, liked to spend money extravagantly. (Only Bryan himself was more extravagant, but that was for a different reason, and after all, it wasn't his money.)

Because Bryan's mother, Vera, insisted on buying my wedding dress, we made a special trip to San Francisco, staying in the Fairmont Hotel (at his parent's expense, of course). Vera took me to I Magnin, at that time probably the most expensive and elegant store in San Francisco. We went to a special part of the store where salesladies brought us various items to try on-- first the dresses themselves and then all the accessories: shoes, purse, hats, etc.

I had never shopped in a store like that before, certainly never been waited on that way. I felt uncomfortable in the situation, but not uncomfortable enough to deny myself a new experience. In the end we (I think the choice was more Vera's than mine) selected an ankle length dress--pink taffeta under an overdress of white eyelet with a pink cummerbund. There were matching pink satin shoes, a pink beaded purse and a small pink flowered hat with attached veil. I didn't see the price tags on any of it except the hat, which was a "Lily Daché", the ultimate headwear designer at the time. As I recall, the price on that was $75--at least ten times what I'd ever paid for a hat. And as if that weren't enough, Vera insisted on also getting me a "going away" outfit--a two-piece black taffeta affair.

One detail which stands out in my mind is that, as I was trying on dresses, one of the salesladies remarked that the gold cross I had around my neck (and which I nearly always wore) wouldn't "go" with the dress. I would have to take it off and instead wear something like a single strand of pearls. To me, though the thought was incompletely articulated at the time, it felt as if taking off that cross was the ultimate symbol of sacrificing my old self. As I recall, when I actually wore the dress for the wedding, I had nothing around my neck.

The wedding was held in the Garden Court of the St. Claire Hotel in San Jose with a justice of the peace presiding. I had tried in vain in the weeks preceding the marriage to somehow manage a Catholic wedding. But the fact that Bryan had been married before, no matter how briefly, seemed to make that impossible. I don't recall being unhappy about the final arrangements, however. It was a lovely setting, I did have a beautiful dress, and it was a small but elite group who attended.

George Harris, an artist and Stanford art professor, was Bryan's best man. Frederic Spiegelberg, who about that time had started up the Academy of Asian Studies in San Francisco with Alan Watts, was there with his wife, Rosalie and their daughter, Corinne. I believe Dan Mendelowitz, another art professor at Stanford and early collector of Bryan's paintings was also there.

The only people connected with me that I remember at the wedding were my mother, Mrs. "J", a woman who lived in my apartment building and who had become a sort of mother confessor to the students in the building, and Betty, my bridesmaid, an old friend from high school. My mother wore a new dark blue suit, hat, gloves, and shoes that Bryan and I had bought her for the occasion.

One person who should have been there but wasn't was Hughes Rudd. He had been in the English Department at Stanford, studying with Wallace Stegner, when Bryan was in the Art Department. I had first met him the weekend we were in San Francisco to pick out the wedding dress. The three of us had gone out together that Saturday night. I remember dragging ("dragging" is the right word) Bryan and Hughes to Mass in one of San Francisco's stately old cathedrals the next morning and enjoying immensely their discomfort at being there. I remember when I first met Hughes feeling some reservations about the hastiness with which I had become involved with Bryan. But by that time Hughes was already spending time with Ann, who was shortly to become his wife.

Hughes, in addition to being a budding writer, was a good photographer and had promised to come to the wedding and take pictures. When he didn't show up (because he was either drunk or hung-over from the night before) we had to grab a commercial photographer from down the street. I'm glad we have some photos of the wedding, but the results were less than I might have hoped for. I never quite forgave Hughes for that one.

My going-away outfit, it turned out, was a waste of money. I came down with a bad flu just after the wedding and spent the following few days in bed at the ranch. By the time I was feeling better, we were involved in day-to-day living and had forgotten any plans to go away.

Although, now that I was married, I had no need to work, I had already signed a contract with the city of Los Gatos to work as a lifeguard and swimming instructor, as I had done the previous year. So through the summer I commuted down the winding mountain road from our ranch to the pool. The more I think about it now, looking back, the more strange I think it must have seemed to Bryan's erudite and sophisticated friends that he had married a swimming instructor!

Fortunately, I don't think any of them knew that in the previous months, while I was going to school, I had been working nights as the box office cashier in a less-than-first-class movie theater in San Jose! Most of his friends were, in fact, quite tolerant and accepting of me. The only comments I was aware of were that I was so young. Actually I was twenty-one, not an early age to marry in those days. But Bryan was twenty-seven and most of his friends were five to fifteen years older than he.

We were scarcely through half the summer when I realized I was pregnant. I hadn't thought to try not to get pregnant. But I certainly hadn't expected it to happen that quickly and easily.

My mother had always said she never tried not to get pregnant (she had never mentioned the word "contraception") and that she was pregnant only once, with me, at the age of thirty. I guess I unconsciously assumed (oh those dangerous assumptions!) that because it had been that way for my mother- -and also because I had been lucky enough not to have been tripped up by any of my various sexual escapades before marriage-- that it wasn't going to happen then either. I couldn't have been more wrong! When we separated five years later, I had had three children and one abortion in those five years. But I'm getting ahead of myself.

*****

I knew, of course, about Bryan's drinking problems, but in the early weeks of the marriage another (perhaps connected) problem became apparent. I had never been so sexually turned on in my life. After all, I was married, sex was an acceptable part of marriage, and I was anxious to experience it as fully as possible. The problem was that, although Bryan wanted to make love and initiated lovemaking, when we actually got down to it, he seemed offended by my enthusiasm. He called me a whore, pushing me out of bed and asking me with great sarcasm what it had been like with my other lovers. Before our marriage he hadn't questioned me about what sexual experiences I might have had with former boyfriends and I had not thought that he really expected me to still be a virgin at the age of twenty-one.

Looking back now, it's easy to understand how his mother's treatment of him as a child had conditioned him to feel guilty about sex. These days one would probably spend a few sessions with a sex therapist and the problem would be resolved. But then I knew of no such solution and was more and more perturbed and frustrated trying to deal with his attitude about sex--in addition to his drinking, my being continually pregnant, trying to take care of children, etc.

There were, in spite of the problems, however, many memorable things about those years. I had been right. I was being exposed to a whole new, and very rich world of the arts. Bryan was, first of all, a very talented painter. But more than that--he knew the history of painting and had the kind of mind that was always collecting minute, exotic details, not just about painting and painters but writing and writers, music and musicians--from Bach to Billie Holiday.

But none of this knowledge was boring or pedantic--at least not the way he presented it. It was more as if you were being told some piece of recent juicy gossip about something or someone extremely important--some very privileged piece of information that was for your ears only.

When I went back to pick up my degree in English after we were divorced, my modern literature instructors were amazed at the things I knew about the personal lives of people like Dylan Thomas and Wallace Stevens--things they hadn't known. It must have sounded as if I had known them personally--and indeed it almost seemed as if I had.

*****

On the Skyline ranch there were three buildings: the partially renovated farm house, a barn about half-way around a road that curved along the side of an apple orchard, and a second barn at the far end of the curve where the road ended directly across the orchard from the house and that Bryan had turned into his studio. Bryan spent most of every day in the studio painting, starting early in the morning and taking a break after lunch to take care of other business. He didn't seem to mind my sitting in the studio as he painted; in fact he encouraged it. He told me early on, "You don't know anything about painting now, but you will." After awhile he would even ask my opinion about where a particular line of a branch or edge of background should go.

When he submitted his first painting to a juried exhibit for the annual at the San Francisco Museum of Art, he let me choose the painting. I was a bit conservative in my choice. Rather than the semi-abstract bird paintings he was working on at the time, I chose an earlier painting he had done of the lake on the Stanford campus, painted in Matisse-like mauves. That painting won first prize that year.

The following year, we each chose one. His choice was one of egrets he had just finished. I can't remember now exactly what I chose, only that my choice again won first prize. His selection was not even picked for exhibition by the judges, which, to me, only proved that my conservative, pedestrian tastes were more in line with that of the judges.

As Bryan used to say, "Nature imitates Art. True art presents to the viewer a new way of seeing, and until we have become accustomed to that new way, we don't really see the painting." I remember one time after we were divorced seeing some birds flash across the sky in a parking lot, suddenly seeing them as if they were a Bryan Wilson painting and realizing what he had meant about life imitating art.

During the years following our marriage, Bryan began to have more and more success with the paintings. The awards at the San Francisco Museum helped, of course. Even the fact that he went to the awards ceremonies drunk and used his time at the microphone to insult the socialite museum supporters didn't seem to hurt. These same socialite ladies made the trip to visit his studio at the ranch and bought paintings, smiling all the while at his sarcastic remarks over afternoon cocktails.

There were shows at the Stanford Museum and, after a short time with another gallery, he joined Gumps' Gallery in San Francisco. We were visited by a curator from The Metropolitan Museum and Charles Alan of the Alan Gallery in New York. I still remember with amusement the strange juxtaposition of urbane New York gallery people discussing arrangements for exhibits while I sat calmly breast-feeding our latest child.

My involvement with the paintings was more than passive appreciation, however. While Bryan was extremely uncomfortable dealing with the business aspect of his work, I loved it. The job of organizing shows, and naming and pricing paintings fell largely to me. It was a good arrangement since Bryan only wanted to paint, not market his paintings, while I enjoyed connecting the paintings, which I had come to truly appreciate, with people who could show and sell them.

*****

Bryan had started his career as an artist early. He told me that when he entered kindergarten, the teacher wanted the children to paint a mural on one of the school walls. According to Bryan, he got the job and spent the whole year doing only that. He probably exaggerated a bit--he always did like to make something into a good story.

In high school he began to work in the style of various early twentieth century painters. The paintings I remember best were done in the style of Picasso's Blue Period. They weren't imitations of actual Picasso paintings, but rather subjects Picasso might have painted and done so stylistically accurately that to probably anyone but an art expert they would appear to be legitimate Picassos. He also, from very early on, had a particular interest in birds and animals. In high school he corresponded with a well-known ornithological illustrator and did many detailed paintings of birds himself.

Later, when he was living in Danville, a small town east of Oakland, with his third wife, he indulged his interest in exotic animals by keeping his own menagerie: Virginia, an Alaskan timber wolf, a mountain lion named Grace, two cheetahs called Serengeti and Ngorongoro, a parrot called Parsley, sundry hawks, and many others I've since forgotten.

Bryan also had other interests not related to the arts, except perhaps indirectly, such as a passion for exotic sports cars. He was an avid reader of *Road and Track*. I think it was the design of cars like the Ferrari Mondial or Siata Spyder that initially appealed to him, but he also enjoyed driving sports cars. In those days you could simply walk into a car dealership and, if you had the right style, could take any car out for a spin alone-- no salesperson in the car with you. It was fun trying out the latest Jaguars, Mercedes, Porsches, etc. though when Bryan came home with his first Porsche, a bright red Speedster, I was sitting upstairs holding our first baby, Bryan Jr., who was just a few days old, trying to breast-feed him with tears running down my cheeks.

Now that so much time has passed, I can understand that Bryan's buying the Porsche was just his way of celebrating a very important occasion, the birth of his first child. He had been extremely proud, if somewhat surprised, when he found out I was pregnant. So although he was awkward about expressing feelings of tenderness, the feelings, I'm now convinced, were genuinely there. It was just that, for me, buying an expensive sports car I knew we couldn't afford didn't seem to be the best way to celebrate the birth of our child.

But, in fact, actually being able to "afford" something, in the sense I had become accustomed to during my years of having just enough to get by on, meant nothing to Bryan. If he wanted something--and he always wanted the absolute best-- he simply bought it, knowing he could get the money to pay for it later from his parents. It was an attitude toward money which was totally opposite from mine and which I found completely incomprehensible and profoundly disturbing.

The ranch we were living on--250 acres--had been bought by his parents. They paid his phone and utilities--we didn't even see the bills. And, in addition to that, they sent Bryan a monthly allowance which they increased when we got married to something over a thousand dollars a month--a more than adequate income in those days for two people who had no mortgage or rent to pay. Except that Bryan bought a lot of steak and lobster and caviar and good wine. But probably our biggest expense was his bar bill at his drinking spot in Los Gatos where he drank only the best Green Label Jack Daniels--and lots of it.

Another expense was clothes. Perhaps we were not really being as extravagant as it seemed to me at the time, but we did shop at the best stores. Bryan would often see a dress or coat on a model he thought would look good on me and insist that I try it on. And, of course, it always suited me perfectly--at that price how could it not!

As a matter of fact, the Porsche was only the first in a string of sports cars Bryan bought and sold over the five years of our marriage. The Porsche, being only a two-seater, worked as long as we could fit little Bryan's bassinet in back of the seats under the tonneau cover. The Porsche was the car I really learned to drive in as Bryan taught me how to corner in true sports car style while going up and down the mountain roads to our house.

But within a year, on a trip to Monterey for the Concours d'Elegance at Del Monte Lodge in Pebble Beach, Bryan suddenly decided to trade the Porsche for a Mercedes 190 SL. It was not much larger but a little more family oriented than the Porsche. That car, however, didn't last long either. About the time we moved to Merced when our second child, Bekah, was five months old, Bryan replaced the Mercedes with a Lancia Spyder followed by another Lancia, a Grand Turismo. And, as if to make up for the lack of family orientation in his choice of sports cars, about that time we also acquired a Volvo station wagon, one of the first to be imported into California.

Even I enjoyed driving the Lancias. After the stiff, somewhat formal handling of the Mercedes, the Lancias, especially the Spyder, which we both drove in Merced auto-cross races, were exhilarating. The procession of sports cars didn't end there, however. Shortly after David, our third child was born, we made a trip to New York. The owner of a New York Gallery had been out to see Bryan's work and we were going to make final arrangements for Bryan to officially join his stable of painters.

It was my first trip outside California, except for going to Reno with my mother as a child. In four days in New York, with the help of a friend who worked in the rare book department at Scribners and had connections, we did more than I would have ever thought possible. Our arrival day included a trip to the Cloisters to see the unicorn tapestry followed by a bus tour of Harlem. The following days and evenings were packed with visits to all the major museums and galleries, shopping at Bergdorf Goodman, a trip to the Greenwich Village walk-up of my old high school friend, Toy, then a budding actress, accompanied by a musician friend of ours who had just had his Carnegie Hall debut. (Somehow during the evening he wound up in Gloria Swanson's neighboring apartment.) We bought lobsters at the Fulton Street fish market and chased them around the kitchen floor daring each other to toss them in the boiling water, had lunch at the Russian Tea Room and beers at P.J. Clarke's. We saw the newly discovered Mort Saul at the Blue Angel and Laurence Olivier in "The Entertainer", even though tickets had been sold out for months.

While in New York, Bryan was phoning auto dealers trying to find an Ace Bristol, since he had decided he wanted to drive one home across country. There were none in New York as they had all been sold for the upcoming Sebring races. However he finally managed to locate one in Detroit of all places. So on leaving New York, we flew to Detroit, picked up our bright red racing Ace Bristol and started the trek home.

The Ace Bristol drew a lot of attention whenever we stopped for gas, but most people thought it was an Austin Healy, that being about the most exotic sports car anybody in the mid-west had heard of in the late fifties. The car was heavy to steer until it got over 80 MPH and only had side curtains, not windows. When we encountered tornadoes in Texas, Bryan and I both had to cover our faces with bandannas to keep the dust out. I wonder what people in passing cars thought of this couple in bandit disguise rolling along the highway in their exotic red sports car. The Ace Bristol never even got home to Merced however. Bryan stopped at an auto dealer's in San Francisco and traded it in for an Aston Martin.

*****

I had made no attempt after we were married to keep in touch with friends from high school or college. I felt that I had moved into a completely different realm of existence. Next to Bryan and his friends, any previous connections of mine seemed like pale shadows. Part of the mystique, I know, was that Bryan's friends were older, but they were also people with more esoteric backgrounds and exotic tastes--people like the Onslow-Fords.

Gordon and Jacqueline Onslow-Ford were living in a hillside house in Sausalito when I first met them. Bryan had met Jacqueline at Stanford, I think, although she was considerably older than Bryan (and also older than Gordon). She had a certain fame as poetess, par excellence, at Stanford and was the heiress to the Johnson Wax fortune. I was told she had met Gordon, a member of British nobility, when he, at that point in the war the naval commander of a battleship off the coast of Mexico, had jumped ship and deserted. The story goes that they spent several years in Mexico during which they were held for a time in the mountains by banditos who threatened their lives and only finally agreed to let them go because of the wonderful stories Jacqueline kept them amused with (a la Sheherizade).

Gordon apparently felt that his real calling was to be an abstract painter, so they had moved to the San Francisco bay area. He set up his studio on a houseboat moored in Sausalito, space shared with Alan Watts and the Greek painter, Varda. Gordon had begun collecting French and Italian painters before the war and had a sizeable collection. Whenever he and Jacqueline needed money for living expenses, they would pull out another DiChirico or Braque and sell it.

I don't know that Gordon ever sold any of his own paintings, but that never seemed to concern him. He was more interested in theorizing about painting and went on at great length about how all painting was simply a series of lines, circles, and dots--precisely what his paintings were--various constructions of lines, circles, and dots.

What attracted him to Bryan's paintings I don't know because Bryan's were, if somewhat abstract, never non-objective, and didn't fit Gordon's theories at all. Nevertheless, the Onslow-Fords became one of Bryan's first patrons, not only buying paintings but also putting us in touch with other people in the art world. I remember particularly a dinner that they gave for the Paris-based Chilean painter, Matta. It was a bohemian gathering in an upstairs room of a North Beach restaurant attended by about fifty of the artistic elite of San Francisco, from painters and writers to filmmakers and astrologers.

Fascinating and stimulating as this life was, the problems associated with continually being pregnant, trying to take care of children with little preparation or emotional support, and coping with Bryan's drinking and other problems eventually became too much for me. We had spent a couple of years in the San Joaquin Valley, first in Merced and then just outside the tiny town of Snelling, because Bryan wanted to be nearer to his mother after his father's death. But feeling totally isolated and out of place in the backwater mentality of the central valley at that time, we decided to move to Berkeley.

We bought a house in the lower part of the Berkeley hills-- a rather grand three story building having an enormous living room with views across the bay to San Francisco, a room that Bryan immediately turned into his studio. That was the only time I know of that Bryan had an actual job besides his painting. He had been hired by the Oakland College of Arts and Crafts to teach painting classes and, in addition to his regular classes, held a Sunday drawing session with a live model in the studio at the house. The teaching job at the college didn't last long, however, as he was less than successful in relating to his students, many of whom left his classes in tears as a result of his harsh criticism of their work.

We had only been in Berkeley a few months when it became clear I was pregnant again, at a time when Bryan's drinking was at its worst and I was feeling that I couldn't take the stress of our strained relationship much longer. I made an appointment with a psychiatrist and through him was able to arrange an abortion at a hospital in Berkeley. This at a time when abortions were illegal in California except in cases of the most extreme urgency. I remember the psychiatrist asking me if I had considered suicide. I told him, yes, I had considered it but thought I would probably choose to leave Bryan first.

Not long after that, Bryan announced one evening that he was going to San Francisco to see his ex-wife, Joan Clay. I was offended and upset. When I was invited later that evening to go for a drive with the brother of a friend of ours from Merced, I was happy to get out of the house.

Mel and I drove around, mostly just talking, and somehow ended up at a part of the San Francisco Presidio where a path crosses just under the Golden Gate Bridge. We were walking along in the dark with only the lights from the bridge above to show us the way and the sound of the waters of the bay lapping at the rocks below us. I remember how comforting it felt to have someone to talk to, someone who did not make witty, esoteric comments but who merely listened and tried to respond in a helpful and sensitive way. The next thing I remember is putting my arms around Mel, kissing him, gently pulling him to the ground and our making love right there in the middle of the pathway. I take full responsibility for what happened, though I don't recall any particular resistance on Mel's part.

The next morning Bryan wanted to know where I had been and what had happened and I told him. That was the only time he ever hit me during our marriage. It frightened me because I had never been struck before by anyone. I locked myself in the bathroom and, when I felt reassured that he had gone, came out and began to pack some clothes. I managed to get myself and the children organized enough to get to my mother's house in Palo Alto where we stayed a few weeks until I could find a place of our own and a job to support us. That was the end of the marriage.

Bryan's violent reaction seemed extreme to me at the time. Now I understand that what I did, given Bryan's sexual insecurities, was the most hurtful thing I could possibly have done. My emotional state was such that I was only reacting to my own emotional needs, not consciously intending to hurt Bryan. I was too immersed in my own problems to consider how my actions would affect him.

In the months following the breakup, Bryan alternated between bringing presents and asking me to come back and threatening me with a rifle and smashing in the rear window of Mel's car parked in my driveway. Even more than ten years later, after Vittorio had arrived from Italy and we were planning to be married, Bryan phoned with threats that he would have Vittorio deported. It seemed to take Bryan's third wife being killed and himself almost dying in a car accident that I'm sure involved drinking for him to sober up in more ways than one. A few months after the accident he phoned, and for the first time since our divorce he was there, present, not full of anger or pretence, but simply a human being.

*****

He hasn't had a drink in many years now. We talk on the phone when something comes up regarding the children and visit occasionally when I go down to California to see the children and grandchildren. He is still very uncomfortable in social situations and large gatherings, even when it's mostly family, but now at least we can joke about it. We both know that when he gets too uncomfortable, he will suddenly disappear, sometimes without even saying good-bye.

As far as I know he still paints every day, and in the last few years has turned out a body of work that is remarkable for its spare clarity. Unfortunately, this later work has never been shown anywhere. He couldn't get along with the people from Gumps any more. Besides, Gumps' gallery is too small to show these paintings some of which are at least five by six feet. He long ago disassociated himself from the gallery in New York and another one he had for awhile in Beverly Hills. He never dealt very well with gallery people. Now, although our son, David, has tried his hand at publicizing the work, Bryan doesn't seem to care about showing or selling the paintings in spite of having gone through a large inheritance from his mother rather quickly and having very little money to live on. The last time we got together when I was visiting the children in Carmel, I tried to talk to him about alternatives for showing his work. He told me succinctly it was none of my business.

As ever, and especially now that he sees his life winding down, so to speak, the only thing that really matters is to paint for as long and as much as possible. Painting has always been his true religion, the only thing he has been single-mindedly faithful to. And he was right when he said that after spending all those hours sitting in the studio I would know something about painting. I do. Enough to be sure that someday, despite his unwillingness to do anything to promote his work, it will be recognized.

Chapter V

Carmel

When Bryan and I separated, I took a job in an electronics plant for a year, partly to have some money to live on and partly to do something routine to recover my sanity. At the end of that year I was so bored with the ordinariness of what I was doing that I decided to return to school, this time to pursue a degree in English. It took two years to complete my B.A. with the new major and another two years to finish my master's degree at Berkeley. On completing the M.A., I was offered a teaching position in the English Department at San Jose State where I had done my undergraduate work.

That first year of teaching was extremely stressful. I was still feeling the pressures I had been under at Berkeley, trying to survive in a harshly competitive graduate program and do a reasonably good job of mothering three children at the same time. By the middle of that first teaching year, when Mel, whom I had been seeing since my breakup with Bryan, finally decided that perhaps marriage was not such a bad idea, I was only too glad to take what seemed to be an opportunity to escape.

Our marriage was actually accomplished by taking a trip to Mexico at Christmas time during which we found out we couldn't be married there after all because the papers from my divorce from Bryan were not in order. Mel, being the ever practical person he was, wanted the marriage to take place before January 1 for tax purposes, so we made an unscheduled stop in Las Vegas on the way home.

I still had the school year to finish out, of course, but by June, I was ready to pack up and move to Carmel where Mel was working.

A few years before, on a visit to Carmel, when I had no thought of ever living there, I had visited Point Lobos State Park. I was standing where the path to Gibson's Beach ended on a cliff by the wooden stairs leading down to the beach itself. I thought it was the most beautiful beach I had ever seen with its golden sand and blue-green waters circled by ice plant covered cliffs. I looked across the beach to where another staircase began on the opposite side and was quickly engulfed in dense bushes. I could just see through the brush and trees what appeared to be elegant old Spanish-style houses. It wasn't actually a wish, because I knew it was too much to wish for, but I was thinking how wonderful it would be to live in a place like that.

When Mel began looking for something we could rent, he discovered that a fellow he worked with was about to move out of a house in Carmel Highlands, just where I had seen those houses on the southern end of Point Lobos. So somehow that unexpressed wish from years before seemed to be taking shape in present reality.

I should explain a bit. When I say "Carmel", I am not referring to the kitschy, too too cute charm that most people associate with Clint Eastwood's village by the sea. The "Carmel" of the residents is a far different place. And where I was living is technically not Carmel at all but Carmel Highlands. I only use the term "Carmel" to refer to the area in general.

Carmel Highlands, called simply "the Highlands" by the natives, is reached by heading down the coast on Highway #1 as if you were going to Big Sur. You drive past the main Carmel exit, past the Carmel valley turnoff and the turnoff to the mission, cross the Carmel River, and continue past San Jose Beach (also known as Monastery Beach for the Carmelite nuns from the monastery up the hill who occasionally walk along the beach in their long black robes and white gull hats). At the end of the beach you enter the dense foliage that marks the beginning of Point Lobos. The house Mel had found for us was just past a ravine that marked the end of the park.

It had originally been built by the current owner's father as a studio! The exterior was stucco with a Spanish tile roof. The living room, the original studio, looked like some of the chateaux I was later to see in France--eighteen-foot ceiling, terracotta tile floors, and a fireplace big enough to roast a whole boar in (something that would have been possible as wild boar do roam the hillsides of Big Sur).

Some of the furniture that had been left in the house included an Italian Renaissance dining table and chairs and a seven-foot armoire that had supposedly belonged to Guy Fawkes. A spindle-edged staircase led up from the living room to a balcony that was also a library whose walls were lined with autographed first editions. A door led into a bathroom, and a further door opened to a bedroom with its own fireplace and more carved Renaissance furnishings.

From the bedroom window one could see across the southern end of Point Lobos the rocky promontory called "Bird Rock" for its congregations of Cormorants and Brown

Pelicans. Looking past that and out to sea at certain seasons one could just make out the hazy spouts and barely curved projections from the water that signaled the annual migration of the gray whale.

Beneath this upstairs bedroom, still in the original part of the house, was a Spanish-style kitchen with floors and counter tops of the same terracotta as the living room. One entered from the dining room through an arched adobe doorway, and below the high ceilings were adobe ledges holding brightly decorated Mexican or Spanish ceramic pots that I assume, like some of the furnishings and the library, had been there since the house was built.

I was often in the kitchen preparing macrobiotic meals for friends on their way to or from Big Sur or making my special dark, heavy bread with its added raisins or apples or other more exotic ingredients to the accompaniment of the latest Beatles or Jefferson Airplane or the local young guitarist who seemed to find thirtyish women immensely attractive.

The other part of the house was a bedroom and attached bath that had been added at a later date. This bedroom, with its own fireplace, built-in bookcases and cupboards, and again a view out across Bird Rock, was mine--and Mel's when he happened to be home.

The house and its setting, however, are only part of what made this an exceptionally memorable period in my life. Just as significant was the time itself. We moved to Carmel in June of 1965. For me it was the mid-point of my life, a mid-point that just happened to coincide with the middle of the psychedelic revolution in California.

1965 was the point at which Alan Watts had already proclaimed the "isness" of Zen and Jack Kerouac had given us a taste for the joys of non-directional wandering. Aldous Huxley had extolled the virtues of the chemically-aided inner search. Esalen, newly created from Big Sur Hot Springs, had become Fritz Perls' center for introducing to the avant-garde businessman and bored suburban housewife the introspection and tactile awareness that was already an essential part of the Big Sur inhabitant's lifestyle.

Mel and I had, for several years, been spending time in North Beach, the area renowned for its "Beatnik" culture in the late fifties. He had friends who owned and worked in one of the main jazz clubs there. One of these friends, the bartender (who was also an artist) ran off to Big Sur with the wife of the owner. By the time we moved to Carmel, they were well established as one of the first of the "Hippie" culture in Big Sur.

In other words, I could not have picked a more opportune time in my life (not that I consciously and deliberately chose it) to move to what was really the north end of Big Sur and therefore, along with the Haight Ashbury, the heart of the psychedelic revolution in California.

I still had three children to care for, of course. But they were at that age between childhood and teenage when they really seemed to care for themselves. There were a number of other children in the Highlands about the same age and I got the feeling that they roved, somewhat like a pack of wolves, from house to house, finding what there was to eat or do until they got bored and then moving on to the next place.

I was teaching a few courses at the community college, but even my teaching style had changed. Whereas in my first year I had always worn skirts and nylons, I now wore pants and sandals to class. I brought into class some of the exercises I had learned from sensitivity training seminars. We had live poetry readings, on one occasion a reading in the living room at my house with Richard Brautigan down from San Francisco as guest poet.

I was continuing to use a semantics text, which meant a lot of discussion about propaganda, prejudice, perceptions and politics, specifically the Vietnam War. I had worried during my first year at State that I might get into trouble with the administration for some of the topics under discussion. Now I was less worried about administrative scrutiny of the radical subject matter in my classes and more concerned about what I saw as the discrepancy between my position as authority figure in class and my increasingly unconventional lifestyle out of class. In fact, just thinking about it often gave me a case of the giggles.

It should be said that the experimentation with psychedelic substances in the early and mid-sixties came from a much different attitude than most of the drug-taking that goes on today. It was not self-destructive or even particularly escapist. Most of us just wanted to explore dimensions of experience that were not easily attained otherwise, and as long as we felt fairly sure that what we were taking was not physically addictive or dangerous, we were willing to experiment.

Mel and I had both smoked marijuana, of course, and tried a number of similar things. But up until that time, although I knew about LSD in some detail from the descriptions of our friend who had moved to Big Sur, I hadn't taken it myself.

One day toward the end of that first summer in Carmel, a friend of Mel's came down unexpectedly from Berkeley with Layla, his Indian princess girlfriend. Mel was not home at the time, but was expected sometime later in the evening. The friend was planning to "drop acid" on the beach, and offered me some. His girlfriend declined, saying she was "allergic" which I took to mean that she had experienced a "bad trip". She offered to be our guru and guide, just in case.

It was one of those particularly warm, perfect, perfumed days with not a cloud in the sky--what other kind of day would you expect in California in the summer? Actually in mid-summer, when it's 90 degrees inland, the fog rolls in along the coast, especially among the trees of the Highlands. But not this day--perhaps it was late enough in the summer.

Because the parents of the current owner of the house had donated the land which formed the southern end of the park, anyone who lived in one of the several houses and cottages on the property had access to Gibson's Beach via a path beginning at the end of the owner's driveway and ending just where I had seen it from the other side of the beach those many years before.

The pathway began opposite an imposing stone house that never appeared to be occupied, at an unlocked metal gate that signaled the beginning of the park. From there the path consisted mostly of stone steps turning and twisting their way through bushes and shrubs and finally arriving at a beach of coarse, translucent, honey-colored sand. We got to the beach and stretched out on the sand, having swallowed our little white pills back at the house.

One moment I was simply enjoying the relaxing warmth of the sand. Then that feeling began to extend itself until I felt myself melting into and becoming part of the sand, all of which struck me as pleasurable and at the same time funny in a cosmically funny kind of way--as if someone were saying, "You think you're so special, so separate and unique, but really you're just another grain of sand!" I rolled over onto my back and looked up at the cliffs, and the ice plant had come alive. I could see it growing. I could feel it clasping the crevices in the rocks as if it were my own hands grasping, digging in with my fingernails. I felt it move and spread, flowering proudly, enjoying the strength and beauty of its own movement while the rocks, too, vibrated with an ancient, massive power.

The clear aquamarine water, its rhythmic white crests undulating toward me and back, was inviting me to join in some sort of dance. Somewhat precariously, I willed my body to lift itself from the sand and propel itself toward the water, which, miraculously, it accomplished. The waves held me in their embrace and cradled me with a gentle, rocking motion. I don't even remember the water being cold (which it surely was, the ocean at Carmel never being anything less than icy!). I seem to remember some sort of animal in the waves with me, though perhaps that was something I imagined. There are sea otters around Point Lobos, so it could have been--I'm not sure. I'm surprised I didn't just swim or get carried out to sea by the current, oblivious as I was to time or circumstance. But I didn't, and eventually found myself back on the beach.

When I was dry and we had done something with our sandwiches (I don't really remember eating them) it was decided (probably by Layla) that it was time to go back to the house.

We started up the same pathway we had traversed on the way down. But it was not the same. At each step and turn, the plants and shrubs held out their branches to greet me, to caress me with their leaves. I could almost hear their greeting as well as feel it. It was as if I had just given some sort of performance. As I was leaving the stage, the audience was reaching out to clasp my hand, to express their appreciation. I felt loved and wanted and had a sense of belonging, as with a group of close and loving friends.

At this point in telling the story, I always stop and look around and if anyone is listening, I check their expression to see if it tells me that, yes, I have finally done it. I have completely overstepped the bounds of acceptable disclosure in the context of social intercourse. They think I am completely out of my mind!

Why then am I telling you this? Why should I expose myself to ridicule? I suppose the reason I want to tell it is the same reason I remember it with such intensity. Nothing in my life before that had ever been experienced so wholly or completely with all my senses, and it gave them such a thorough shaking up that although to most people I may appear quite normal, and technically (medically speaking) am, the outer fringes of perception are always there.

But to continue my story--when we finally got back to the house, I talked with some of the flowers in the garden and discovered again, as I had with the sand and rocks and other plants on the beach and pathway, that I was not alone or separate from other things--that we were all equal and part of some quite amazingly beautiful whole.

The rest of the day was a series of revelations, from staring at a large pointillist painting of concentric circles and being sucked into the middle of its galaxy, to experiencing with the five-year-old child of another set of friends who had dropped by, the totally self-absorbed sensual concentration of eating ice cream.

I remember looking at myself in a mirror and seeing through my skin, as if it were transparent, a physical body at a certain stage in the aging process. I remember thinking that it was not pretty but worthy of respect because it was a gift, or rather a sort of loan or wardship, something one had a responsibility to care for because it was the self's means of communication with others.

Taking a shower I discovered a hurt place on my foot and responded with an objective tenderness, as one might respond to a child being hurt, understanding that being hurt is an opportunity to grow, learn, and develop a sense of compassion and caring for others.

All right, "so what?" you might say. What good has this sort of insight done for those of us who experienced the sixties in this way? Are we any wiser, more enlightened, more prepared to make changes to improve the world we live in? For that matter, is the world any better now than it was in the sixties? Some would say worse--more violence, less adherence to "family values".

I suppose it depends on your point of view, your background, your general outlook on life. I can't speak for others. For example, our friend from Berkeley and his girlfriend were much more extreme politically than I was. They disappeared shortly after that day to join some sort of subversive underground movement dedicated to sabotage--you know, like blowing up things. If you were to hear them describe what went on that day, you would probably not even know it was the same day I was talking about.

I can only say that for me that period of the sixties, and perhaps that day more than any other, was what Joseph Campbell would describe as a "peak experience", a watershed, a turning point. The insights that I encountered that day were perhaps always latently there, and perhaps in many ways I have been rediscovering them ever since. But that was the day on which they were most forcefully present, not merely to the intellect, but to my entire being.

I stayed in the house in the Highlands two years. But, like the psychedelic revolution itself, it was an experience too intense to continue for any length of time. During the spring of '67 I had spent time wandering through the Haight Ashbury and going to concerts at the Filmore auditorium. All the hype about the warm, loving, beautiful people seemed to be true. I still have a clipping someplace of Herb Caen's column in the San Francisco Chronicle reviewing the Monterey Pop Festival in June of '67. His title was "A Warm and Groovy Affair". And indeed it was. But by the time I returned from Europe in the fall of '67, the atmosphere was already changing.

My departure for Europe in June was a fitting end to that particular period of my life. Mel and I were at the Monterey Pop Festival most of the weekend before I left. I still vividly remember Janice Joplin's performance. As I was returning to my seat from getting something to drink, she started singing. I stopped where I was standing, drink glass in hand, and stood still, mesmerized, for the rest of the performance.

Mel and I went to the football stadium later that night because it was rumored that both the Beatles and Stones were in town and would turn up for an impromptu performance. Nothing of that sort happened, but I still remember watching all the tired festival goers stretched out in their sleeping bags listening to the Doors' "Light My Fire" being broadcast from the back of a flatbed truck. It had an almost eerie serenity which was to be echoed a little over a year later when, on a ferry late at night en route from Palma Majorca to Barcelona, I would once again be surrounded by hippies in sleeping bags and the sounds of the same music being played on someone's boom box.

Sunday afternoon's schedule was a concert by Ravi Shankar, with baskets of orchids being tossed through the audience. Since, to me, anything after that would have seemed anticlimactic, I opted out of the evening concert. Though I was phoned about three that morning by a friend wishing me "bon voyage" and telling me I had missed a great performance by Jimi Hendrix.

I didn't miss Jimi Hendrix completely, though, as he and his entourage were on the same early morning flight I was taking from Monterey to San Francisco and then on to New York. I still remember the stunned expressions on the faces of other travelers at the San Francisco airport that morning at the sight of those wild looking, fantastically garbed musicians.

So June of '67 ended my stay in Carmel Highlands. I returned, of course, first to stay for a short time with Mel in the house he had rented in Big Sur and then later to Carmel proper. But those two years in Carmel Highlands were a unique experience that could only have occurred in that time and place under those particular circumstances. I'm just glad I happened to be there.

Chapter VI

Lerici

Je n'aurai pas le temps,
pas le temps....
De visiter tout l'immensité
d'un si grand univers.
Méme en cent ans
Je n'aurai pas le temps
de tout faire.

Michel Fugan

I left Carmel for New York via San Francisco on the Monday morning after the weekend of the Monterey Pop Festival, stayed in New York long enough to see another concert in the East Village and then caught a cheap flight from New York to Luxembourg.

There was a bus connection provided by the airlines for the hour or so trip into Paris. The bus had a sound system and, as we bounced along the autoroute leading to Paris, I heard a melody that caught my attention. It was a new song by a popular French singer of the period, Michel Fugan. I could only catch a few of the words then, but later, when I had managed to decipher most of it, the song seemed to express many of my feelings about that time and situation.

"I will not have the time", it said, " Even running as fast as the wind, as fast as time, even flying, I will not have the time to visit all the immensity of so great a universe. Even in a hundred years, I will not have the time to do everything." Even though that song registered strongly with me at the time, I could not have predicted how much more true its words would seem years later.

When I arrived in Paris, I registered in a six-week course at Alliance Française. A Parisian friend I'd met a few years before in Carmel had given me his sister Anne Marie's name and phone number in Paris and she introduced me to people and places I would never have discovered on my own. Actually, because her English was better than my French, she was one of the few people I spoke English with during my two months in Paris. Other than that I tried to avoid English speakers whenever possible and to blend in with the crowd on the left bank. It worked well enough that I was often stopped by tourists asking for directions--in French.

When the course was over, Anne Marie helped me arrange the purchase of a red VW bug, gave me some tips on staying in hostels, and suggested an itinerary for my first tour outside

Paris. I began my wanderings with a visit to Chartres, Normandy, and Mont Saint-Michel and, after a brief return to Paris, began the longer and more adventurous part--the chateau country, the Dordogne, Nice, and finally Italy.

I was staying in hostels, partly to save money and partly because, traveling alone, it was a good way to meet people and learn more about the places I was in or was on my way to. Having the VW, I was in the enviable position of being one of the few hostellers with transportation and soon began checking the hostel bulletin boards for people who wanted rides in the direction I was going.

By the time I left Nice for my first excursion into Italy, I had in tow a Scotsman and a British couple who had been involved in several film projects including the making of "Blowup". Our first stop was San Remo on the Italian Riviera, and the second was Lerici.

Lerici seemed to have been there forever. It was a tiny fishing village on the coast a few kilometres south of La Spezia. The castle on the promontory at the south end of town, which served as a tourist attraction during the day and a youth hostel at night, dated back to the thirteenth century. No doubt hundreds, maybe thousands, of tragic, happy, wonderful, even important historic events took place there. I know of none of them. For me Lerici was less a place than a point in time that would mark another major change in my life.

How I happened to be there was strange in itself. I'm not sure I even remembered the name, but I couldn't forget the picture on the postcard I had received in London during my first trip to Europe in 1962.

My excuse for going had been that I'd been accepted to attend a "Four British Universities" summer session, and I was determined to make the most of the opportunity. I could have chosen Oxford, Edinburgh, or Stratford, but chose London to be more at the center of things and where I could see more theater. Then I chose the most round-about way to get there-- plane to New York, the Leonardo Da Vinci, (one of the last grand transatlantic liners) to cross the Atlantic, a day's stop in Naples (just long enough for a tour of Capri), disembarking at Cannes, five days split between there and Nice, by train to Paris for five more days, and then finally to London.

The Lerici connection had really all started on the Leonardo. I was having a shipboard romance with a man from New Jersey. He was the ex-husband of an obscure American jazz singer and was traveling with his parents and teen-aged daughter back to live in Italy where the family was originally from. A girl I shared a dining room table with, a student at some posh eastern college, was having her romance with the tourist-class bartender who happened to be from the little town on the coast of Italy I now know as Lerici.

When I went to London for my six weeks stay at the university, she went with Guiliano to Lerici, which was how I happened to have that postcard--that scene of ancient, crumbling, majestic buildings overlooking the most blue, serene, inviting sea I had ever seen--perhaps even more inviting after a few weeks in cool, gray, drizzling London.

I couldn't go to Italy then. After all, my raison d'être for being in Europe at all was my course at the university, and after that, well, I had obligations at home. But I kept the postcard, and even if I hadn't, the picture was there in my mind just waiting for the right time, some five years later, in the summer of 1967, when I would once again have figured out some clever excuse to get myself off to Europe for another summer.

This time my excuse was that I wanted to study French. Having taken some French at university, I wanted the opportunity to immerse myself, at least as much as was financially and otherwise feasible, which meant the length of a summer. But perhaps beyond what I was stating as my reason for going was the simple call of adventure, the sixties' insatiable quest for new experiences.

We arrived at mid-day and, leaving the VW in the hot sunshine of the parking lot below, ascended the hundreds of stairs up into the heart of the castle. We passed through the damp coolness of what seemed to be former dungeons, and abruptly entered the brilliance of the castle ramparts. They seemed deserted except for one girl rinsing her hair under the single cold-water tap that served as the hostel's water supply and cursing in German because she couldn't get the soap out. Her only audience was another blond girl lounging on the ramparts in a bikini and a macaroni necklace.

The office was closed (normal for a hostel office at mid-day) with a note saying (in Italian) "Will be back at four, Buddha". So we changed into our swimming gear and retraced our steps through the castle to the beach below.

By suppertime, we had officially checked ourselves into the hostel. The hostellers, who had dispersed during the day to the beach or sightseeing in town, began to reassemble. Hostel visitors usually prepare their dinners side by side in the hostel kitchen, either on their own or in small traveling or nationality groups. At Lerici, people tended to congregate in international groups, specifically including those who had just arrived, to head to one of the local restaurants for dinner.

I was approached by someone who identified himself as Mario and asked if I wanted to join the group. I said I needed a few minutes to change. By the time I was dressed and outside the women's dorm, Mario had disappeared. Instead, another young Italian was there who introduced himself as Vittorio and said he was going down to the restaurant with the same group and would be happy to show me the way.

Our group at the trattoria numbered about twelve or thirteen, including Buddha, the hostel manager. There was the usual excellent pasta and good red wine and animated conversation in several languages including Italian, French, German, and English. As I recall I was the only native English speaker, but a number of the Italians knew some English and wanted to practice. So I managed by being able to follow the conversation in everything but German, and by speaking English or French.

After dinner, the group broke up, people going in various directions for the usual after-dinner promenade. Vittorio asked if I would like to stroll along the pier where the fishing boats were tied up. So off we went, arm in arm, Vittorio talking continuously in his broken English, telling me things about the town, about Italy, and finally about himself.

I can't remember now exactly which things I found out then through a roundabout confusing sort of conversation and which things I think he must have told me because I now know them. He said he had been born in Naples, had grown up in Savona, a bit north of Lerici, and that he was a student of Classics at the University of Naples. The thing I remember most clearly was that in response to my polite inquiries about his family, he looked up at the sky and said in a sad voice, "My father is a white dove". Fortunately I knew enough Catholic theology to catch his tongue-in-cheek reference to the "Holy Spirit" and its supposed responsibility for the pregnancy of the Virgin Mary.

It was also then or sometime in the next few days that he produced from his wallet the photo of a young dark-haired girl holding a chubby bright-eyed baby of about nine months. I understood that the baby was his and that he was not married to the girl. Later I heard the story of how his mother had taken care of the girl while she was pregnant. But he hadn't married her because, as he said, he didn't love her. I have no idea what pressures might have been brought to bear on him to marry her. But knowing now what I didn't know then--the whole story of his mother's pregnancy--I understand why she took the girl in and cared for her--regardless of what Vittorio decided to do.

My relationship with Vittorio progressed rapidly from conversation to intimacy. This was the 60's after all, and I was a traveler in Europe like so many others in search of whatever adventure might present itself. Vittorio, it seemed, was another adventure, a way of experiencing Italian culture that would otherwise not have been possible.

After four or five days, it seemed time to travel on to the next hostel, although in this case it wouldn't have been necessary. The usual hostel stay was limited to four or five days. But because Vittorio, like several others there, was a good friend of Buddha's, he could make special arrangements for friends to stay longer, having already been there most of the summer himself.

When I mentioned to Vittorio my plans to leave the following morning, he seemed agitated. He asked if, since I seemed determined to leave, he could go with me, saying in his sad and heavily accented voice, "I love you." I wondered what he meant. I thought of my visit to Lerici and my encounter with Vittorio as being just one more interesting interlude on an adventurous summer excursion around Europe. I wondered why this impetuous young Italian student had decided he wanted to come with me. The Scotsman who had arrived with me was coming along as far as Florence, and since the British couple had made other plans, I had room for two more. Vittorio found a woman who wanted a ride to Pisa, and the following morning we headed south.

At each stop, Pisa, then Florence, then Venice, I thought I would be leaving Vittorio behind, but he stayed with me. Soon he was the only one with me and was driving my car in grand Italian fashion so that I was hanging on to the sissy bar and saying small prayers as we went along. Still, it was better than doing all the driving myself, especially when he kept putting his foot on mine on the accelerator to make me drive faster or kept running his hand up my leg as I was trying to drive.

When it came time to cross the border into France and head back to Paris, he again wanted to come along. By the time we arrived in Paris, Vittorio had convinced me that hitchhiking was much more fun than driving. I had a friend newly arrived in Paris who was delighted to take over my car for the week and then drive it to Le Havre for shipment to New York. So Vittorio and I used the next ten days to hitchhike through Chartres to Biarritz, through Burgos to Lisbon, south to Malaga and then back again via the Alhambra to Madrid where we caught the night express into Paris.

When Vittorio finally saw me off on the bus to Luxembourg to catch my bargain-fare flight home, I was in a state of complete exhaustion. I was glad to be going home and glad to be seeing the last (I thought) of Vittorio. If you had told me then that within three months I would be back in Europe with my three pre-teen children having given away everything I owned with the intention of going to live with Vittorio in Naples, I wouldn't have believed you.

I wouldn't have believed that the next time I stayed at Lerici with Vittorio I would have my three children with me or that, a few years later, I would pass that way again with Vittorio, my husband, and our two-month-old daughter.

Chapter VII

Lydia

That first evening with Vittorio strolling along the pier of the tiny fishing village of Lerici I asked him the usual polite questions about his family. He responded in his heavily accented English, eyes upturned in a gesture reminiscent of a Raphaello angel, "My father was a white dove." The story of his mother, as I was gradually to discover over the next few years, was much more complicated.

Lydia Garbarino was born in September 1914 in the seaside resort of Mondello just outside Palermo, Sicily. Her father, originally from northern Italy, was the "Prefect" of Palermo, a sort of quasi-judicial government appointment, and the family lived in the villa that came with that position. I don't recall actually seeing the villa, but from having visited Palermo and Mondello, I picture it as spacious and grand, its many high-ceilinged rooms sparsely but elegantly furnished with carved dark furniture, its courtyards filled with fountains and Bougainvillea.

From what I've been told and from seeing some old family photos, I know that Lydia grew up in an atmosphere of affluence and gentility. It was an atmosphere in which a very intelligent girl, headstrong by nature, might have developed ideas and attitudes not generally associated with young girls anywhere in Italy at the time, particularly in Sicily. I have no way of knowing anything about the politics of the family when Lydia was a child. I do know, however, that Lydia, her sister Licia, and their brother all became dedicated Communists. Since the early Communists were usually freethinking intellectuals, I suspect their family had a somewhat different notion of the place of women in the home and society than was prevalent in Sicily at that time.

Whatever the reason, Lydia was not married off young in a socially-approved, family-arranged marriage, though she was traditional enough to have worked on the items for a trousseau. The carefully embroidered sheets, pillowcases, tablecloths, and yards of handmade lace sitting in a suitcase in my closet are evidence of that. Instead, she entered the University of Naples. And more than that, she chose to study architecture--hardly an occupation that would have been considered acceptable at that time for a woman! Her final degree, upon graduating, was perhaps some combination of Arts and Architecture, at least it was something that gave her the necessary credentials to teach art at the middle school level, a compromise she perhaps had to make in order to have any sort of work at all.

I've seen photographs of her with her fellow teachers at that period. She is a tall woman, standing very straight, unsmiling, large breasted but not feminine, in fact somewhat masculine looking with her hair pulled back sharply and her prominent aquiline nose. I have also seen oil portraits done of her some years earlier by her art professors in which she appears much softer, almost pretty. But even in those more flattering portraits, one can see the unmistakable pride that would later, perhaps in self-protection, become what one might describe as haughtiness.

She was thirty when she became pregnant by a physician and surgeon in Genoa. She was teaching in the Italian Riviera town of Savona. It must have been unusual in Italy at that time for a woman of thirty to be single. Still, the usual arrangement would have been for them to marry as quickly as possible. There seems to have been some initial reluctance on his part, at which point the families, at least hers, got involved and tried to push for a marriage. However, as I understand it, her pride prevailed, and although he finally consented to marry her, she refused.

She returned to Naples where Vittorio was born in October 1944. How she got there is something of a mystery in itself since during that period (mid-1944) the country was divided into separate zones, the Allies controlling the area south of Rome and the Germans controlling everything to the north. Presumably she would have had to pass through the combat lines of two armies to get from Savona to Naples, a task that I have no trouble imagining her accomplishing by simply talking and bullying her way through the two command posts.

By the time Vittorio was born and she was ready to return to work, the war was just ending. Italian soldiers were returning home, and jobs that had been held by others were now patriotically being given back to the returnees. Teaching was no exception. When Lydia wanted to return to work after Vittorio was born, she had to face the problems of raising a child on her own without the benefits of child care or any organized support system and ostracism from society for having had a child under those circumstances in the first place. She had to take whatever part time jobs were offered. I say, "had to" but, given the family circumstances, I think it was, again, more for reasons of pride than economic necessity.

While she traveled on crowded buses between two or three part-time jobs in different sections of Naples, Vittorio stayed with his grandmother in Caserta, the town sprung up around the king's summer palace just outside Naples. Or at least he stayed there most of the time except for the occasions when he would share a cramped room in Naples with his mother, sleeping in a makeshift crib created out of a dresser drawer. When he was old enough to go to school, he spent more time with his mother, often returning home from school to the empty room where he learned to fix snacks of bread fried in olive oil and salted.

He was only eight when she had her first breakdown and was hospitalized. Why was he not sent back to stay with his grandmother at this point? Had the grandmother died? Was she not well enough to care for him? For whatever reason, he was put in some sort of institution--convent, orphanage, boy's school--where he stayed during the time she was in the hospital. He was taught a trade--tailoring--I suppose because most of the boys in a place like that would have had no opportunity for schooling beyond the first few grades, if that, and needed training for work. He learned how to blind stitch a hem in a way that even I, who had done a lot of sewing and some tailoring, didn't know. He was also, probably for the first of many times while his mother was hospitalized, exposed to what we would now call sexual abuse. I don't know that from anything he has told me but rather by implication from the patterns of behavior that unfolded during our marriage and from what I now know about sexual abuse.

I doubt whether his mother would have known about any of this. When she was at home and working, her main concern, aside from her work, was that her son do well in school. After the usual elementary program he was sent on to the "Liceo Classico" that the elite few attended in preparation for a university education in the Classics. He studied nine subjects including Latin and Greek and passed the exams given each year by outside examiners with top marks. I'm sure this was achieved not only because of his natural intelligence, but also because of his mother's pushing and prodding. It must have been especially important to her that her son succeed, in the same way that her own accomplishments had been important. Even more so, given the continual difficulties and social rejection they faced.

So, as he was growing up, and she was achieving some degree of recognition for her competence and dedication as a teacher, there were still times when she was placed in the hospital. What had she done to be treated that way? When I first met Vittorio I asked him what sort of behavior had more recently caused her to be hospitalized. He told me she kept the shades down during the day and would only go out at night to buy bread and other necessities. He told me she read several newspapers every day, was particularly interested in politics, and often got into political harangues, even with strangers. He told me she bought lots of shoes and had many pairs in the closet she hadn't even worn. And sometimes, when the weather turned nice in the spring, she would ride her bike down to the wharf where the fishermen brought in their catch and talk to them as they worked. For these things they locked her up, forcibly gave her medication, and if the medication wasn't enough to keep her from struggling to get out, they would tie her to her bed until she was quiet.

*****

My first encounter with Lydia, the first time I met her face-to-face, was in the summer of 1970. I had met Vittorio in the summer of 1967 and that winter had returned to Europe with my three pre-teenaged children, having some typically sixties notion of adventurous romance. We rented a summer flat in Lucrino, just north of Naples, and were there for two tumultuous months until the Italian Army caught up with Vittorio, whom, along with other rebellious students, they had been trying to draft. During that two months we sometimes stopped by the apartment Vittorio had previously shared with his mother. Vittorio went in while I waited in the car with the children. When he came out, he usually had a wad of lire bills he would toss into my lap saying, "My mother says 'these are for your whore'."

So it was not until after Vittorio had come to California and we had been married in the summer of 1969 and our daughter had been born in May of 1970 that I actually met Lydia.

Vittorio had preceded me to Naples by a couple of weeks that summer. It was necessary for him to go ahead because, by that time, Lydia was permanently in mental hospitals. He could take her out at any time as long as he guaranteed to be responsible for her and see that she took her medication regularly. So he needed to first find a suitable place for them to stay and then go through the piles of paperwork necessary for her release.

He had found a pleasant enough basement suite in an old building in Caserta. It was reached through a massive entranceway which, fully opened, would have been big enough to drive a carriage through. There was a dry dirt courtyard and a simple wooden door opening into two rooms with only the most basic wooden furniture. One room had a single bed, table, and chest of drawers. The other was furnished with several straight-backed chairs and a two-burner wood stove for heating and cooking.

Vittorio picked us up at the airport in Rome (me and Nicole who was barely two months old), and after a night at a hotel, we drove to Caserta. I remember the heat and brightness of the courtyard and the contrasting coolness and darkness of the apartment. Lydia was sitting quietly in one of the chairs and didn't rise as we entered. Vittorio didn't introduce us. He simply took Nicole from my arms and placed her in those of his mother.

Nothing was said. Lydia didn't smile or comment. She held Nicole and looked deeply into her eyes. For several long moments Vittorio and I stood and watched while his mother held the baby. Then slowly she handed the baby back to Vittorio, got up and began to bustle around getting a fire started in preparation for cooking, all without having acknowledged my presence in any way.

That was the summer I met Lydia's brother and his wife. They also lived in Caserta, and Vittorio and I went to visit them one evening. They had a fairly ordinary apartment and, as I recall, a couple of grown or almost grown children. What was memorable for me about the visit was that although the brother would mention Lydia when his wife was out of the room, it was clear that her name was not to be mentioned in his wife's presence. Vittorio explained later that because his aunt was afraid or ashamed of her sister-in-law's mental illness, she tried to pretend Lydia didn't exist. I also seem to remember some discussion about a family ring they said Lydia had, but that they felt was rightfully theirs.

That summer we stayed in a hotel nearby for a while. Then, when Lydia seemed to be managing well enough on her own, we left. We first traveled south to Taranto at the instep of the "boot" of Italy, then to Brindisi and by ferry over to Corfu, visiting with Lydia again briefly just before coming back to the States.

Generally she would be all right on her own for a period of time. Then at some point, perhaps because she had stopped taking her medication, or simply because she felt the urge to do something and didn't give a damn what other people thought, she would call attention to herself or provoke someone and, because of her previous history, would once again end up in a mental hospital.

When we arrived the next summer, we found her in one of the hospitals in Naples. I had seen the inside of one private mental institution in California up to that time, but nothing could have prepared me for the shock of entering that hospital in Naples. My first impression was of long gray hallways, with grinning or scowling pajama-clad inmates pushing long empty trolleys that rattled and echoed on the bare marble floors. Going down one corridor there were windows on one side and periodic doors leading into open courtyards with straight-backed wooden chairs and large picnic-type tables. Across the courtyard was another door that, as we entered the courtyard and came closer, I could see was a dormitory with rows of stacked double-decker metal beds.

I had noticed, as I sat in the car outside waiting for permission to come in, the number of people, mostly hunched-over old women dressed in black, carrying baskets draped with what appeared to be table napkins. Now I saw that these baskets contained a sort of picnic lunch that the family member or members were sharing with their relative inmates.

Once inside the courtyard, the place didn't seem so bad until I began to hear moans and cries from inside the dormitory and was informed that certain of the inmates had not "behaved" and therefore had been shackled to their beds, an experience

Lydia was apparently familiar with. The people in charge all seemed to be nuns as was apparent from the traditional black habits they wore. According to Vittorio, it was doubtful whether any of them had any training in psychiatric nursing.

As we sat in the courtyard talking, the nuns came by frequently offering to share food that other visitors had brought or to bring us a coffee. They came by so often and interrupted the conversation so much that Lydia became irritated and told them the equivalent in Italian of "get lost!" On one of our visits that summer, the day after our car had been broken into and all our possessions stolen, one of the nuns came around selling colored posters of saints. When we said we weren't interested and the nun kept persisting, Lydia flew into a rage, jumped up and tried to tear off the nun's headgear, at which point she was restrained by several other nuns and finally led away.

I also remember another incident that happened perhaps a week later, after we had been there several times for visits. Vittorio had requested and received permission in advance to take his mother out for the afternoon. We had planned to go for lunch somewhere and then for a drive. We arrived as scheduled and Lydia was ready. We left the area where her courtyard was, went down the long hall, and prepared to sign her out. Then it seemed there was some sort of problem. The desk clerk didn't have the papers with the right authorization. The person in charge of the hospital had to be found which took some time while we waited by the desk. Finally a tall, official-looking man in a business suit came down the hallway. He was smiling and polite, ready to apologize for the mix-up. But Lydia would have none of it. She pulled herself up to her full height, which came close to matching his and certainly outdid him in sheer presence. She launched into a lecture that, though my understanding of Italian was imperfect, the tone and diction made clear was an eloquent condemnation of the stupidity and inefficiency both of the hospital and of himself personally. Judging from the expression on his face, it was a confrontation in which he was no match for his adversary.

A few years later, when Nicole was four, I was once again in Italy, Vittorio having traveled on his own the previous summers. Again Vittorio had gone ahead, gotten his mother out of the hospital, and found a place to stay, this time in the tiny seaside town of Caprioli, about 150 kilometres south of Naples. The place he had rented was in a not quite finished apartment building a short distance from the beach. There were two unfurnished rooms we used for sleeping and a bathroom with a fancy modern toilet and washbasin. The only problem with the bathroom was that the shower nozzle in the ceiling reached everywhere in the room so that all towels, toilet paper, etc. had to be removed from the room before taking a shower. There was a fair-sized porch that looked out across the road in the direction of the beach though the house across the way obstructed the view. The porch had several chairs and a table, and an adjacent alcove had been supplied with a wooden table supporting a two-burner gas stove. We did our dishes in the bathroom sink. There was no refrigerator but, in spite of the heat, that didn't seem to be much of a problem as Lydia shopped every day for our vegetables and meat which Vittorio supplemented with what he caught fishing from rocks along the coastline.

Shortly after I arrived, we moved to the basement of the house across the street. It again had two rooms, this time with real beds--mattresses on iron spring supports-- and a similar kitchen--only this one had a sink. There was also a refrigerator--in the bedroom. There was no bathroom but rather a toilet in a sort of shed across the courtyard that the proprietor with a great flourish supplied with a toilet seat on our arrival "for the American lady". He also hooked up a shower nozzle (cold water only) on the outside of the building near our courtyard entrance which could, by hanging sheets on the adjacent clotheslines, give enough privacy to be used as a shower.

Lydia insisted on doing all the shopping and cooking, though occasionally I would be given some simple task such as stringing the green beans. She, for the most part, ignored me, assuming that I was incapable of knowing what to shop for or how to prepare it. She was pretty much right. I wouldn't have known how to select the best tasting, though not necessarily the largest, plumpest, most colorful, from an unfamiliar variety of vegetables or how to make the simple, delicious soups and pasta dishes she created.

So while she treated me with benign neglect, and continually argued with Vittorio about what seemed to me the petty details of when and what we should eat, most of her attention was focused on Nicole. When she went shopping she wanted to take Nicole with her, which she did until we found out that during these excursions she was stopping for visits along the way at which Nicole was being indulged in all the traditional Italian "dolces", something we as health-conscious North American parents abhorred. She also insisted on feeding Nicole with the traditional maternal encouragement to "mangia", even though Nicole at that age was perfectly capable of feeding herself. She even took charge of Nicole at the beach introducing her to other children, wading with her, and toweling her off after she had been in the water for what Lydia considered enough time.

When she wasn't busy with one of these activities, she went to the local bar. By "bar" it must be understood "bar" in the Italian sense of a place where coffee, liquors, soda pop, cigarettes, and often also snack-size meals are sold. This one doubled as a corner grocery, with a small supply of canned goods and a counter displaying cold meats and cheeses. There were three or four tables with chairs usually occupied by older men drinking wine and engaged in endless games of cards or dominos. Occasionally a woman sat tentatively perched on a chair while wiping up the continual spills from a small child eating ice cream. But Lydia was the only woman who sat there for long stretches of time the way the men did--and not only sat there but joined them in their games, a glass of wine at her side and a cigarette dangling from her mouth. This obviously eccentric behavior, however, seemed to be accepted with good-natured humor by the locals.

It was less than an idyllic summer in that Vittorio and I were continuing a prolonged argument that had begun even before we left California. Many times our discussions or arguments lasted until very late at night. The main dissension between Lydia and me arose from the fact that Vittorio often wasn't anywhere around at mealtime, and when I was sent to look for him, couldn't find him. This was a situation for which, in Lydia's eyes, I was entirely to blame.

The only time the tension actually erupted into the kind of shouting match between me and Lydia that frequently arose between her and Vittorio was shortly before we were due to leave. As I recall, it was another one of those times when I had been sent to find Vittorio for a meal and he, as usual, was nowhere to be found. Lydia was yelling at me for not being able to find him. I, perhaps having been in Italy long enough to have become acclimated, felt free to yell back, half in English and half in Italian.

The time came for us to go, leaving her, as usual, on her own until such time as she stepped far enough out of line to be returned, once again, to the hospital. Lydia and I were both still feeling a certain amount of hurt and animosity so that there was a coldness in our farewells that day. If only I had known that was the last time I would ever see her, or the last time she would ever see Nicole, I would certainly have made more effort to set aside our petty quarrel and give her a hug and some words of affection or encouragement. But, being caught up in the feelings of the moment, I instead said a polite, rather formal farewell as Vittorio and I headed for the train station.

About two summers later, after we had moved to Vancouver, Vittorio was off to Italy once again. His mother was back in the hospital. This time she had been put there presumably because she had gone to Bologna where her sister lived. They apparently got into some sort of spat, which seems to have involved a vase being thrown, Lydia being the thrower and her sister the recipient.

About that visit I know very little. Vittorio had been gone several weeks and had written telling me that he had, once again, gotten his mother out of the hospital. I believe this time they were staying in or near Genoa where Lydia had friends, a former student of hers who had married a bank manager.

What I do remember is getting a phone call from Vittorio in which he was very distraught and almost incoherent but from which I understood that his mother was dead, that she had taken her own life and had done it in such a way that for days they didn't know where she was. Eventually, it was Vittorio who found her.

That was about all I was ever to know. When Vittorio returned to Vancouver several weeks later, he didn't want to talk about his mother's death. In the six or seven years after that, until we finally separated, her death was only discussed once.

A friend was over one evening who had some background in therapy and, for a change, Vittorio seemed to be willing to talk about what had happened to his mother. He began by talking not about the way she had died, but about the funeral. It had been difficult to arrange as Lydia had not been a practicing Catholic and had committed suicide. But the main point came when he described his aunt (the one married to his uncle in Caserta) insisting that the ring that Lydia had on not be buried with her. His aunt tried over and over unsuccessfully to dislodge the ring from Lydia's finger. In the end, though Vittorio didn't say exactly how, except for the suggestion that something like a knife was involved, the ring was removed.

I assume the ring in question was the one I'd heard argued about years before in Caserta. But if that ring was the same, I have reason to believe the aunt was still unsuccessful. Included in his mother's possessions that Vittorio returned to Vancouver with that summer, were paintings of her and a few she had done, a few vases and busts, an ornate crucifix, and an antique ring--one diamond surrounded by several smaller ones set in a combination of yellow and white gold. The clasps holding the diamonds, I've been told, need replacing before the ring can be worn without danger of losing the diamonds. It was suggested, when I had it appraised for insurance purposes, that perhaps a better solution would be to put the diamonds in a new and modern setting. But that suggestion offends me. It ignores the whole history, meaning, intricate personal connections, even the tragedy that it is connected to. For the moment it sits in a safe deposit box waiting for a time when Nicole will be the one to make the decision about what becomes of it.

Chapter VIII

Vittorio/Europe

Dai diamanti non nasce niente
dal letame nascono i fiori.

"Via Del Campo"
Fabrizio de Andre

Since I came to Vancouver, the question I'm most often asked when someone hears I'm from California or that I've lived in Carmel is "Why did you decide to come here!" When someone hears my last name for the first time, I'm usually asked in some variation of embarrassed, awkward or even slightly denigrating tone, "Isn't that an mmm--ITALIAN name?" "You don't look Italian." The implied question being, " How did you come to have that name?" To both questions I usually respond, "Well, it's a long story."

After meeting Vittorio in Italy in the summer of 1967, I returned to California. Mel, to whom I was still technically married, had moved from the house in Carmel Highlands to Garapata Canyon in Big Sur. It was only on reflection, and in the process of telling Mel about my travels and about meeting Vittorio, that I began to realize that the events of the summer were not to be shaken off lightly. It had been more than a mad summer adventure. Something about Vittorio had become lodged in the core of my being and would not be dislodged. Each of Vittorio's letters, written in his fractured and at the same time poetic English, only served to intensify the feeling.

By early December I had either given away, or packed in boxes for Mel to keep, everything I owned, and, with Mel's blessing, flew to Europe with my three children aged ten, eleven, and twelve intending to start a new life in Europe with Vittorio. The children and I stayed in London long enough to see the sights, then went on to Amsterdam where Vittorio was arriving to meet us.

We were in Amsterdam about a week, spending time with friends of mine from San Francisco, an artist and his designer wife and staying in a hotel on the edge of Amsterdam's infamous red light district. Vittorio took us on a tour, explaining to my children and to me what all those ladies were doing sitting in display windows.

I think what the children enjoyed most about Amsterdam was going down to the street outside the hotel early in the morning and collecting the coins that the drunks had dropped the night before on their way to or from visiting the prostitutes.

Vittorio did some quick shopping around and found a second-hand Opel station wagon in good enough condition to get us to Naples. Our first stop was Paris where the children's main activity was running the elevator up and down--until the manager put a stop to it. After that, we stayed mostly in hostels, which the children enjoyed, especially Bekah, because the young students in the women's dorm treated her as if she were one of them. She liked one of the hostels so much, in fact, that when it was time to leave, Vittorio had to physically carry her to the car because she had decided that she had had enough of traveling and just wanted to stay at the hostel.

We went through Lyon, then turned east heading toward the Alps. We hit snow in the mountain passes, and even though it was late at night, the children wanted to get out and play in the snow (an exotic sight for children from California!). Vittorio prevailed, however, and we pulled into Torino some time after midnight.

When we finally arrived in Naples, our first job was to find a place to stay. I had thought that in Vittorio's letters when he spoke of his "house" he meant "house" in our North American terms. I soon realized that in Italy there were no such things as houses in the American sense. People lived in what we would call "apartments" or what the British would call "flats", a flat taking up an entire floor of a building, and a few of the very wealthy lived in what would be called a "villa". What he had referred to as his "house" was actually a small apartment he shared with his mother, not a place where he could take me and my three children.

Having no furniture, we needed a furnished apartment and finally located one we could afford in the summer resort area of Lucrino, about thirty minutes north of Naples. It consisted of a bedroom, bathroom, kitchen, dining room and small living room with a couch. Vittorio and I had the bedroom and Bekah took the couch, leaving the boys, Bryan and David, to manage as best they could with their sleeping bags in the dining room.

Aside from the lack of beds, the biggest problem was lack of heat. Because the apartments were normally rented only during the summer, there was no heat source other than the oven. We managed to get a "bomb", a large propane tank with heater attached that we placed in the center hallway. But being a flat, with windows in all rooms, the "bomb" only heated the hallway and because it was winter (and Naples can be very cold in winter!) we spent most of our time in the hallway huddled around the heater.

We made the trip into Naples every day for one reason or another. We were either shopping for groceries, trying to find a place to get laundry done, lining up for international gas coupons, or getting gas for the car which, despite our efforts, it was continually running out of. We also had some mechanical problems and when we were directed by several people to an auto mechanic, the mechanic turned out to be an eight-year-old boy.

But my strongest memories of those trips in and out of Naples were of funerals, processions of ornate funeral carriages drawn by four to six large black horses, of line after line of gravestones set out for sale, and also of prostitutes.

There were several street corners, usually in semi-industrial sections, where groups of prostitutes congregated. Unlike the downtown areas where slim, elegant, beautifully dressed prostitutes usually worked alone, watched over by their pimp sitting in a car parked across the street, in these lower class areas, the prostitutes were mostly overweight, with enormous bosoms and tight skirts slit up to reveal fleshy thighs. Until that time I had always thought that Fellini's portraits of prostitutes were caricatures. I now knew it was just factual reporting.

The children, naturally, found these women warming themselves around their oilcan fires to be quite fascinating. They asked Vittorio to explain what those "ladies" were doing there. He responded bluntly, "Those aren't ladies, they're whores."

The problems with day-to-day existence seemed magnified in this strange environment for several reasons. First was the language problem. I only knew a few words of Italian and the children none at all. Although they became friendly with some of the local children, there was none of the free movement from one play area to another that they were used to at home. They tended to play right in or immediately outside our apartment. Bekah's friend, a girl of about ten, was limited in her ability to move around because she was permanently in charge of a baby brother less than a year old who had to be taken everywhere with her. The children seemed to be with us all the time.

We tried, of course, to get them settled in a school. The logical choice was the John F. Kennedy School that was mostly for children of American army personnel stationed in Naples and where, therefore, classes were in English. However, when we took them to see the school and they observed students all in uniform standing at attention beside their desks, my children, being the typical laissez-faire Californians that they were, refused en masse to attend.

There were also other more subtle problems. I was undergoing a culture shock of my own. I was introduced to two couples who were friends of Vittorio's. I remember going for a ride with one of the couples one day from their apartment, which was at the top of a hill, down into town. For some reason the passenger seat had been taken out of the car so that, with Vittorio's friend driving and Vittorio and I sitting in the back seat, his friend's wife was forced to squat in the space where the passenger seat should have been. It was a steep, winding street and Vittorio's friend was driving as fast as he could, deliberately throwing the car around corners to make it as difficult as possible for his wife to keep her precarious balance, all the while laughing at her efforts. He also found time on the way down the hill to tell us about his latest favorite prostitute in the local park and her abilities in performing specific sexual acts. All the while, his wife never once complained or even stopped smiling.

The other friends of Vittorio's were a family with three young children who lived in a small apartment, the balcony of which was the children's only play area. The husband was a businessman of some sort who was seldom home, and the wife was very young looking and attractive. Vittorio told me that a short time before, the husband had gotten another woman pregnant and had brought her home for his wife to look after until the baby was born. He had also about this time gambled away whatever assets he had, leaving the family practically destitute.

One evening the four of us had planned to go out dancing, and the young woman had arranged for a babysitter. Vittorio and I arrived at the appointed time to find the woman beautifully made up and dressed to go out. We waited for her husband to arrive. When more than an hour passed and he was still not there, she dismissed the babysitter. After some two hours he finally came home and without even an apology announced that he was too tired to go out anyway. Again there was no sign of anger or even disappointment from his wife. She seemed to shrug the whole thing off as if it meant nothing, even though I got the impression from Vittorio that this would have been a rare and special occasion for her.

If these two wives did not react to what I considered completely outrageous and unacceptable behavior on the part of their husbands, I did. I was thoroughly offended. I asked Vittorio why on earth they would stay with these men. The answer was that in both cases they were financially and socially dependent on their husbands.

In Italy at that time there was no such thing as divorce, so there was no possibility of remarrying and no chance of having another relationship without being ostracized from society. There was little chance of them finding jobs to support themselves, so they would most likely have had to return to live with their parents. But worst of all, in the case of the woman with the three children, if she had left her husband, she would have had to give her children over to her husband as it would have been deemed that only he was financially able to care for them. There seemed to be no such concept as "child support", much less "alimony".

It was quite clear that in Italian society women were inferior creatures with little or no rights. I had known, of course, that such situations existed in various parts of the world, but to come face to face with it was, for a free-thinking, independent, North American woman like myself, quite a shock. Vittorio seemed to neither defend nor criticize the situation. For him it was just "what was".

A short time later, though, something happened which was even more disturbing on a personal level. One night Vittorio went out to visit some "friends" and didn't get home until nearly morning. I wasn't berating him so much as trying to find out what he had been up to. He cried and called himself a "pig". He told me he had been at some sort of party at which he was being teased, presumably for being faithful to an "American woman". There was some sort of sexual wager, which he lost. It was all a bit vague and certainly very foreign to me--much as if I had suddenly stepped into the middle of 8 1/2 or La Dolce Vita.

The next morning I packed the children and myself into the car leaving Vittorio to sleep off his excesses of the night before. It seemed that in the nearly two months in Naples we had seen practically nothing in the way of tourist attractions. I had heard about the beauty of the Amalfi peninsula, so that was where we went.

I couldn't believe even by the time we got to Sorrento that we could have been in Naples so long and missed all this. It was so beautiful--the ancient buildings clinging precariously to cliff sides, the spectacular view from the road down the steep cliffs to the crashing surf below. We stopped for lunch in Sorrento and later in the afternoon took a walk on the beach at Positano. I remembered reading a story that Hughes Rudd, Bryan's friend, had written about Positano. He had visited there during the war when people were still living in the cliffs in the hillside above the town. It seemed like a strange connection to be making, with North America and Bryan and Hughes seeming worlds away, and yet knowing that Hughes had also been there.

I wasn't sure what I was going to do when I returned to the apartment, though I was certainly considering packing up our things, leaving Vittorio, and heading back to France. But as was to happen many times yet to come, Vittorio managed to win me over with his apologies, promises, and abject contriteness, and I stayed.

It wasn't long though before I knew something was wrong with me. I had a period that just didn't stop. Vittorio took me to see a local doctor who prescribed some kind of pills that did nothing at all. I was beginning to get worried and also to feel a bit weak from loss of blood.

At about the same time, Vittorio found out the Italian army was looking for him. That winter had been a time of student demonstrations at various universities throughout Europe. The Italian government had decided to deal with the situation by revoking all student deferments, and Vittorio's name was one of those on a list of students who were to report at once for active duty. Actually he had been on the list for some time, but because he was first meeting me in Amsterdam and then living with me in Lucrino, he didn't get the notices they were sending him--or just didn't tell me about them.

At any rate, in light of his need to report to the army and my health situation, Vittorio and I decided to put the children on a flight back to stay with their father in California. In retrospect it now seems obvious that I should have been on that flight too, but somehow I hardly even considered that option.

We saw the children off at the airport in Rome, returned to the apartment and packed all our possessions into the station wagon. Then we drove to Salerno where Vittorio was to catch his train for Palermo, his basic training assignment. I saw him off, drove to the nearest hostel on the Amalfi peninsula just north of Salerno and collapsed for a couple of days until I thought I had the strength to begin my drive north to France.

Along the autostrada heading toward Rome, cars with young men in them kept passing me. The men were leering and making gestures, then slowing down, forcing me to pass, then going through the same routine all over again. At first I couldn't figure out what they were doing. Then I realized that this was the first time I had driven a car alone in Italy, and to make matters worse, the car had foreign (Netherlands) plates.

On the outskirts of Rome I had a flat tire. I was unsure what to do at first but had only been there a few minutes when a jeep containing two young soldiers screeched to a halt. I was thankful for their kindness thinking that Vittorio, now also a soldier, would surely extend the same kindness were he to come across a woman in trouble on the road. One of the soldiers changed the tire and then explained, at least as I understood it, that he would direct me to a nearby gas station where I could get the tire fixed. The other soldier returned to the jeep while the one who had fixed the tire indicated he would ride in my car, the better to direct me to the gas station.

It was clear as soon as I started driving, however, that he had other things on his mind. His reaching across to put his hand on my leg made it clear he was thinking about more than being a Good Samaritan. Being sick and exhausted, my mood quickly shifted from thankfulness to anger. I knew by then that in Italy women are not supposed to take offence at that sort of thing. The proper course of action is to treat it as a joke, smiling and bantering all the while firmly extricating oneself from the situation. I was in no mood, however, to play their cultural games. I pulled the car abruptly to the side of the road and told the young man, "Get out!" Even though I said it in English, which he probably didn't understand, my meaning was obvious, and he got out, looking a little sheepish and embarrassed.

It was only a short distance to the Rome hostel where I had stayed several times before and felt relatively at home. I checked in, told them something about the situation, and was given permission to drive my car, still fully loaded with household goods, into the inner area behind a locked barbed wire fence as a precaution against the omnipresent thieves. I checked the bulletin board and found a young man, British I believe, who was heading toward France the next day and could help me drive my car.

The next morning, on the advice of some concerned members of the hostelling association, I made a stop at an international clinic, Clinica Salvador Mundi, intending to just check with a doctor before heading toward France. The doctor examined me, heard my story, and promptly ordered me off my feet and into a hospital bed. The young Englishman was told to take my car back to the hostel for safekeeping as I was likely to be in the hospital for several days.

It turned out to be ten days. They did a D&C but never did figure out exactly what was wrong. What was wrong by that time, however, was that I was extremely anemic. So the smiling and ever patient nuns kept feeding me and giving me iron supplements. Toward the end of the ten days, they even let me take slow walks in a peaceful tree-filled park across from the clinic.

By the time I was finally well enough to go, though still quite weak, I had phoned the airlines office and made two tentative reservations. One was home to San Francisco. The other was to Palermo, Sicily, where Vittorio was stationed.

Of course, I first had to do something about the car and its contents. I made arrangements with the hostel to move the contents of the car to a storeroom in the hostel, then found a traveler who was happy to pay me a nominal amount to take the car off my hands. I took what I could carry in a suitcase and got a taxi to the airport. I hadn't actually made up my mind which of the flights that I had reserved I was going to take until I arrived at the airport, at which point it became abundantly clear. I was going to Palermo.

It was March, and hot and muggy in Palermo. Vittorio found a hotel for me and was able to get away from the base often enough so we could spend time together sightseeing around Palermo. Visiting with me at the hotel also gave him the opportunity to take a shower.

According to Vittorio the showers at the base were sporadic. One could get all soaped up only to have the water go off completely for the next four to five hours. And the need to take a shower was aggravated by the fact that, despite it being hot in Palermo, the new recruits had all been issued winter uniforms consisting not only of very heavy wool pants and jackets, but also thick wool overcoats and berets, all of which they were required by regulation to wear in public at all times. After a week in Palermo I got a flight to Nice where again I returned to a familiar hotel and rested for a few days before continuing to Paris.

I knew that the friends I had visited with in Amsterdam were now situated somewhere just outside of Paris. Terry had rented a house in a small town about twenty-five kilometres east of Paris and, although Marsha was temporarily back in the States, another friend from San Francisco was staying at the house and I was invited to stay also. The house was mostly just a place to sleep as we drove in Terry's 2CV into Paris every day.

There had already been student demonstrations at the Sorbonne, and I strolled over to the Sorbonne to see for myself the armed police patrolling the perimeter of the university. It was only a day or two after that, as I was sitting outside a café between the Sorbonne and the Seine, that someone yelled and everyone started running. I followed along, not sure what was happening, but soon noticed a burning, smarting sensation in my eyes. It seemed that some of the students had started tearing up cobblestones from the streets and throwing them at the police, or as the students called them, "les flics", and the police were responding with tear gas.

What started that day became a regular occurrence in the days to follow. Fortunately Terry had made friends with one of the students who had "inside" information about where the demonstrations were scheduled for the following day. However, the plans sometimes changed, and we often found ourselves either swerving to avoid cobblestone missiles and tear gas while driving into Paris or else surprised by the sudden distinctive sound of police sirens and long lines of black police vans entering the "quartier" where we were that day.

My first reaction to the situation was to be curious, not frightened. I actually felt quite safe. After all, I was just an American tourist, not a French student. I pictured myself pulling out my American passport in case I got caught in a police rush. It wasn't long, though, before I had observed several of the police-students encounters and realized that the police were not carefully checking national identity cards before hitting people over the heads with their truncheons.

In fact the fellow from San Francisco who had been staying at Terry's failed to return to the house one evening. We were worried and tried to check with the police and hospitals. About three days later we got a call from him in San Francisco. It turned out he had been caught in one of the riots, had gotten his head bloodied, and as soon as he was released from emergency, had taken a taxi to the airport and a flight home. He asked us to please forward his clothes and other belongings.

Terry, being the artist and outrageous adventurer that he was, was not intimidated in the least. In fact, a few weeks later, when I was out of Paris, Terry and his student friend took advantage of some LSD tabs I had left in my suitcase (having brought them with me to Europe just because I didn't know what else to do with them) to get high and then chase after the police vans shooting at their tires with a dart gun.

Meanwhile Vittorio had been transferred from Palermo to a base in the Italian Alps, and I was getting letters in which he sounded sad and lonely and begged me to join him there.

By that time France was under a general strike. All trains and buses were shut down. The autoroutes were free, however, as the tollbooths were closed. I decided to hitchhike, following Vittorio's directions--first south to Lyon then east through Grenoble and when I had crossed the Italian border near Sestriere, I was to begin looking for the uniforms of his unit. All went fairly well according to plan. A short time after we crossed the border I began to recognize the red tie and lion insignia on soldiers directing traffic along the road. I finally asked to be let out so I could identify myself and get further directions.

My Italian was limited, but I knew how to say the equivalent of "I'm looking for infantryman Garbarino". Finally I found one soldier whose face lit up with recognition as he responded while stroking his chin, "Si, con la barba." Knowing that Vittorio was one of the few recruits who wore a beard, I was pretty sure I was in the right place. The soldier rang a number on his walkie-talkie, and I could hear a faint voice at the other end that I recognized as Vittorio's. He said he was "up in the clouds" "near heaven" and that he couldn't wait for me much longer. He gave me some directions that seemed to indicate taking some sort of train into the sky. I didn't understand, but the soldier with the walkie-talkie did and directed me further down the road where I discovered a sort of aerial tramway that did, in fact, seem to go up into the clouds. I bought my ticket and ascended the mountain.

When I reached the end of the ride, there seemed to be only one place to go, a large white two-story building a few hundred meters down a dirt road. As I approached it, I saw people sitting in deck chairs on the front veranda, covered in blankets as the air up there was quite crisp and there were even traces of snow still on the ground. Then I saw some nuns moving about and came to the conclusion it was a hospital. I wondered what terrible thing had happened to Vittorio that he was in a hospital here and tried to locate him by asking one of the nuns. After much confusion on both our parts she finally understood what I was doing there and I understood that this was a T.B. hospital, that he was not there, and that to find him I must follow the dirt road still further up the mountain.

After walking another two kilometres up the road and through the trees into what seemed to be an absolute wilderness, I rounded a bend in the road and abruptly found myself surrounded by army tents and makeshift barracks and soldiers going about various mundane tasks. They were at least as taken aback as I was, seeing a woman, obviously a foreigner, wearing a miniskirt and carrying a suitcase wandering into their remote encampment.

Vittorio was quickly located and almost as quickly told by his commanding officer to get me out of the camp and back into town. Vittorio was even given a leave of several days to take care of me. In the few days that I stayed there, Vittorio and I hiked through Alpine meadows bursting with flowers, explored a ruined castle on the mountainside and even wandered into a complete but deserted Alpine village where we found only a shepherd and his flock that were passing through.

Vittorio, at this point, was having the opposite problem from that of Palermo. He had been issued a summer uniform in place of the winter uniform he had worn in Palermo and, at this altitude, was having a hard time keeping warm.

Shortly after I got back to Paris, a friend arrived from California who was in Europe for the first time and wanted a "tour guide". We rented a car together and returned to some of the locations I had visited previously--Chartres, the Loire Valley and the Dordogne. When we got as far as Nice, we turned the car in and got a flight to Palma Majorca then a ferry to Ibiza as some friends of hers had a place on Ibiza and she wanted to visit them. We found the friends gone temporarily but stayed several days anyway soaking up the sun and enjoying the clean white beaches and crystal blue waters.

When we left, she caught a flight to Madrid and from there back to San Francisco. I took the ferry to Barcelona and then a long train trip along the French coast and down the coast of Italy to Genoa where Vittorio had been permanently stationed.

The rest of the summer was spent going between Paris, where I could stay at Terry's place and observe the progress of the student demonstrations, and Genoa, where I stayed in the hostel and spent time with Vittorio.

By August I knew it was time to get back to California so I could find a place to live and get the children started in school. I returned to Carmel and found a little house near Carmel Woods School. The rest of the year was just a matter of waiting for Vittorio to get out of the army and join me in California, except for two weeks spent with him in Milan at Christmas time.

In Milan, we went together to the American consulate where he filled out his application for a tourist visa to the U.S. saying he only intended to visit and was definitely not planning to stay and swearing an oath that he "was not now nor ever had been a member of the communist party". Both of these statements were, of course, lies, first because he was a card-carrying member of the Communist party in Naples and second because we intended to get married as soon as he arrived in California.

Actually, he was able to get out of the army a bit ahead of schedule as they counted the time they spent looking for him in Naples as time served.

So Vittorio arrived in San Francisco on the fourth of July, 1969, looking tired, malnourished, and more than a little bewildered. I wonder now what he was thinking or feeling when he arrived that day having decided to leave his country, his mother, and his friends to start a new life in a country where he hardly knew the language much less the customs, and where he was planning to take on the responsibility of a wife and three teen-aged step-children.

Chapter IX

Vittorio/California

When Vittorio finally arrived in California, he had, of course, had practice communicating with me in English. It was another matter communicating with my friends and other people he met. The problem wasn't for him to be understood; that he could manage, even though his expressions were often ungrammatical to our ears. He insisted that we were the ones being ungrammatical because he knew from Latin what the construction should be in English and was defensive when actual practice didn't match his expectations.

However, his ability to understand what was being said around him was what caused the most difficulty. In social situations he often gave odd responses to people's questions or failed to respond entirely because he hadn't understood. He dealt with the situation by doing most of the talking himself, something my friends didn't seem to mind as his comments were usually witty and perceptive, if a bit unusual. Some of my women friends even said, only half joking, "Next time you go to Italy, please bring back one of those for me too!"

All in all, he seemed to adjust better than one might have expected. He got along well enough with the children, and except for being a little too forward, one might say flirtatious, with my female friends, he generally fit in. The flirtatiousness one could excuse as simply being characteristic of an Italian. Besides, some of my friends were European or, like Marsha and Terry, had spent time in Europe and were biased in favor of those with European backgrounds.

For example there was Yolanda, originally Italian-Swiss, who looked like a gypsy with her dark hair and long skirts and who could be seen hitchhiking along Highway #1 with her youngest baby, the blond Carolina, on her hip. Yolanda and Vittorio understood one another immediately whether in Italian, French, or even English, the understanding being more cultural than linguistic.

Then there were René and Charlotte, he a Parisian and she from Montreal. It was René's sister, Anne Marie, who had helped me when I first arrived in Paris and who had given me the tip about hostels that had led to my meeting Vittorio. René insisted on taking Vittorio to a rodeo in nearby San Juan Bautista shortly after his arrival. I would never have thought of such a thing, rodeos not being exactly the sort of cultural event I favored, but I think Rene was right. What better introduction to California than a rodeo in a small Mexican-American community.

The reception he got from my mother-in-law, Bryan's mother Vera, was not so welcoming. The relationship between Vera and me had always been strained. She had been widowed when Bekah was still a baby and used the money her husband had left her in what I considered a very ostentatious manner. She always had a new white Cadillac with powder blue upholstery, played golf at the country club, and was an avid shopper.

I found it impossible to carry on a conversation with her as, when she came into a room, she never sat down for more than a few seconds and talked continuously but never seemed to listen. By the time she left, having taken the children out for lunch or dinner at an expensive restaurant and having brought more new clothes for them than they could ever possibly need, ordered often as not, from the best New York department stores, they were hyperactive and I was exhausted.

On the positive side, though, I have to admit she did help out financially. Not that I asked her to. But when it became apparent that Bryan was not going to pay child support, she stepped in and supplied the $300 a month he was supposed to be paying. She also saw that we were stocked up on groceries whenever she came over. But her most generous contribution was buying a house for us.

Being used to "making do", I had found a charming little house to rent when I returned from Europe. At the edge of a ravine, it had a porch the length of the house that faced into the trees. There were no bedrooms, so Bekah and I slept on twin couches in the living room and the boys had cots under the overhang on the deck. We were quite comfortable there, but as far as Vera was concerned it was not good enough for her grandchildren. She suggested that I look around Carmel for a house suitable to buy. I finally found one a little further up the hill.

It was on a sloping lot with the main floor at street level and a lower floor that looked out onto a woodsy back yard. The main floor had a fair-sized living room, a bedroom, bath, and a kitchen with eating area. Downstairs was one large sort of recreation room, a bath, and a laundry room. I could see the potential: all it needed was a deck off the living room to take advantage of the view through the trees and an expansion of the downstairs to make more room for the children. Vera simply wrote a check to pay for it. We had just moved in a few months before Vittorio's arrival.

Even if I had mentioned something about the possibility of Vittorio's joining us in Carmel, and I'm not sure I had, she hadn't heard it and was completely caught off guard by the appearance in the house of this strange-speaking, dark-haired foreigner. Shortly after he arrived, she announced that she would not allow him to live in the house with the children, so Vittorio and I moved out temporarily and she moved in. That arrangement didn't last long, however, as it wasn't all that convenient for her to live in someone else's house (though nominally hers) and, beside that, she began to see that Vittorio and I were serious about staying together and were, in fact, making arrangements for a wedding.

Vittorio picked the date for the wedding (August 25) as it was the anniversary date of our meeting. It wasn't to be a big affair (after all it was my third marriage), but we did want to have something nice to invite all our friends to participate in. We selected a small Episcopalian church in Carmel Valley, and Vittorio found an Italian jeweler in the valley to make matching silver rings for us.

Marsha was my only attendant and wore one of her own design creations--a long Alvin Duskin knit. I was offered a similar choice but chose instead a short dress as being more practical, something I could wear after the wedding.

Vittorio made a special trip to North Beach in San Francisco to buy cannoli to go with the champagne. We almost had a local guitar player booked, but at the last moment he couldn't make it, so we managed with a recording that ended up being forgotten until after the ceremony.

Once we were married, the next order of business was to get Vittorio a permanent residence visa so he could work. That required many trips to the immigration office in San Francisco and filling out innumerable forms. We ran into a glitch when we discovered that Mel had failed to file the final divorce papers, so technically either I was a bigamist or Vittorio and I weren't actually married, something we remedied with a quick ceremony by a justice of the peace in Pacific Grove.

Vera and I had already talked about what renovations the house needed to make more room for the children. I found a contractor who drew up the plans and because he needed someone to help him, Vera was finally convinced to allow the contractor to take on Vittorio as his assistant. (Now that we were married her moral objections, at least, were no longer valid).

So Vittorio's first job in the New World was that of carpenter. His natural intelligence and good coordination made carpentry skills easy enough to pick up, though I don't know that he had had any previous experience of that sort in Italy. Perhaps it was the combination of being good at working with his hands and extremely patient. He even used scraps of lumber from the renovation project to fashion pieces of household furniture.

When the renovations were finished, he applied for a job as gardener at the prestigious Highlands Inn. It was a job that particularly interested Vittorio because the gardening staff brought in plant species from all over the world and did their own plant propagation. He already knew many of the plant genus and species names in Latin and seemed to feel a real tenderness and affection toward plants.

He almost didn't get the job because the elderly, very fussy, and eccentric owner of the inn didn't like Vittorio's beard (at least that was his stated objection). He actually interviewed the two of us together and tried to convince me to convince Vittorio to shave it off. I persisted in saying that I really preferred men with beards. I think my, by that time, obviously pregnant state and the fact of Vittorio's being a new immigrant needing to support a family finally convinced him to give Vittorio the job.

Vittorio developed a strong rapport with the head gardener from whom he learned a great deal and within a few months our newly renovated house had the addition of many large exotic plants as landscaping. Vittorio supplemented this hands-on horticultural experience with night courses at the local community college. He was also taking other courses, some just for fun, like Russian, and others, like English composition and sociology, to improve his English and prepare to complete his B.A.

He was taking the English course with an old friend of mine, someone who had been in a Chaucer seminar with me at Berkeley. The first few compositions Vittorio wrote for this course I read over and found I could hardly even help him because his way of using the language was so confusing as to be almost incomprehensible. I despaired of his ever being able to write in English well enough to pass the course, much less go on to get a degree of any sort. But he persisted. He wrote and patiently rewrote, and eventually passed the course.

I had been working too, doing substitute teaching for all four local high school districts, and in fact had a long-term appointment at Pacific Grove High School that would have lasted until the end of the school year except for the fact that I was expecting the baby sometime in May.

It seems that I had gotten pregnant quite soon after Vittorio arrived. We hadn't tried to prevent my getting pregnant because Vittorio wanted to have at least one child of his own, and I didn't mind the idea. The other children were into their early teens, and the idea of having a baby again had a definite appeal.

In the year leading up to Nicole's birth in May, 1970, we had settled into a sort of family routine, the children busy with school and with their friends, Vittorio occupied with his work gardening during the day and taking classes at night, and me teaching and doing my preparation-for-childbirth classes with Vittorio once a week.

One might have expected some opposition from the older children to having competition from a new baby in the house, but I never saw any such thing. They were intrigued with this new little creature and took turns playing with her and showing her off to their friends. Even her naming was an event in which they were very much involved.

When Nicole came home from the hospital a bare twenty-four hours after she was born, we hadn't quite decided on a name, so we held a family conference which included Laura, a friend of Bekah's. We discussed various names including Michelle, my current choice. I don't remember who suggested Nicole, but when it was brought up, Laura asked Vittorio what the meaning of the name was. He said it was the Greek version of his name in Latin and that it stood for "victory of the people". That decided it; her name was to be Nicole with Michelle as the middle name. Not only did it seem appropriate to name her after her father but, although it wasn't mentioned, what better name for the daughter of a card-carrying Communist.

I had another reason. I intended to call her Niki for short which for me was a reminder of an occasion a few years before when I had encountered the sculptor, Niki de St. Phaille, at the estate of a friend of Yolanda's outside Paris. Nicole remained Niki until she entered pre-school in Santa Barbara at which point she came home one day and announced that she was Nicole, not Niki. So it has remained ever since except when she returns to Niki as a nom de plume or nom de peintre or when someone she has just met calls her Michelle for no apparent reason as so often happens.

Even in those early years in Carmel there were some hints of dark clouds on the horizon, but I tried my best to ignore them. Having made my choice and being in my protectively maternal state, I didn't want anything to disturb what was for the most part a happy relationship. I tried to ignore the sexual innuendos that came up between Vittorio and other women. I tried to believe it was just a generous gesture when Vittorio returned after midnight from his horticulture class saying he had driven a fellow student home to Big Sur.

When my daughter, Bekah, came to me obviously agitated one night as I was cooking dinner and told me Vittorio had pushed her down on the bed and tried to kiss her, I felt as if I had been given a hard kick in the middle of my stomach. But I wanted to believe what Vittorio told me--that he was "just kidding around" and that she was taking it much too seriously. The incident passed, nothing more was said, and there were no further incidents of that sort for the time being.

Meanwhile Vittorio had successfully completed his courses at the community college and been accepted at U.C. Santa Cruz. He continued to work part time while commuting the forty some miles to Santa Cruz and was now officially majoring in Classics. This was his first real opportunity to test himself at the North American university level. His command of English had improved rapidly although I still proofread his papers. When he completed the B.A. program in Classics, he had high enough marks and strong enough recommendations to be offered a fellowship for the Master's program at U.C. Santa Barbara.

If Santa Cruz had offered a Master's program in Classics, we could have continued to live in Carmel, and Vittorio could have kept on commuting to school. But since he had to go elsewhere for the Master's degree and because he had the fellowship offer at Santa Barbara, we decided to move.

The problem was what to do about the older children. Nicole was three by that time and the others were sixteen, seventeen, and eighteen. Bryan had dropped out of school the year before and Bekah was in the process of dropping out. They were both attending a continuation school instead. We could stay in student housing in Santa Barbara, but student apartments were hardly large enough to accommodate a family like ours.

We finally decided to take David with us as he was the youngest of the oldest three and still had two years of high school to complete. The other two were left on their own in the Carmel house. After all, it was really the children's house, Vera having said all along that she was buying it for them. She was already paying something for their support. It was just a matter of putting the telephone, gas, and electricity bills in her name and having her come over a bit more often to check on them.

Besides, I had another motive for planning it that way. Bryan hadn't been any worse, I suppose, than the average teenager, but he had certainly had his share of wrecking cars that Vera bought for him and was just as prompt to replace and had had his minor brushes with the law (as had Bekah). Bekah, on the other hand, had been more of a problem for me. She had developed an "attitude" that made it difficult for us to get along. So while she and Bryan were getting more than their share of attention, David was getting less.

David had always gotten less of everything from Vera. It was as if she doted on the first child because it was her son's son and the second because she was a girl and she could buy things for a girl she couldn't for a boy. But by the time David came along she had lost interest. He got fewer toys, less clothes, and when he turned sixteen, the age at which she had bought new cars for the others, he didn't get a car, not even a used one. I had tried to counter this favoritism by treating the children all equally, thinking that was the right thing to do.

At this point I thought it was time for a change, time to give David some special attention. This seemed like the ideal opportunity to have David as the only teenager in the house,

Nicole being so much younger that she was not a competitor for the more adult companionship he needed.

Bekah has told me many times since that she felt abandoned by my leaving her and I accept the fact that for her, at least, and probably for Bryan too it would have been better to keep the family together for at least a bit longer. (Though my own experience was that of being entirely on my own at almost the same age, with no grandmother supplying a house to live in or paying my bills.) But I don't regret my decision as far as David was concerned. He managed to graduate with his regular class from his high school in Santa Barbara and has since gone on to finish undergraduate and graduate degrees. Perhaps even the close relationship we have had, especially in the last few years, comes from that chance to spend two years having him as the only teenager in the family.

The two years in Santa Barbara were fairly uneventful. Vittorio was doing well with his Master's program. David was getting along at his high school. Nicole was in the university day care part time and making lots of friends with the other children in student housing. At first, I couldn't get a teaching job because of a teacher surplus in the Santa Barbara area. So I spent the first year doing various volunteer jobs and making connections so that, by the second year, I was teaching at the city college.

There were even then some signs of problems that were to assume more serious dimensions later. First, it was already becoming clear that Vittorio's interpretation of some classical writers, in particular Greek comic playwrights, differed greatly from other members of the Classics Department. In fact, there seemed to be a clear split in interpretation, those with Anglo-Saxon, Northern European backgrounds on one side and those with Mediterranean backgrounds on the other. The problem seemed to arise in interpreting some of the more overtly sexual scenes and lines, the Anglo-Saxon contingent preferring a conservative translation and accusing the others of simply having filthy minds for their more blunt interpretation. Vittorio and the Greek professor at the university thought the others were being a bit prissy or at least naive.

The other problem was of a more personal nature. The summer after our first year in Santa Barbara, Vittorio announced that he was going off to Italy again as he had the previous summer. I realized, of course, that he had good reason to go, knowing that he needed to see how his mother was doing and take her out of the hospital for at least a while. What bothered me, I think, was his enthusiasm for going. I felt a little left out, as I had the previous summer. And especially given his behavior toward my women friends, women students in the Classics Department, and women in general, I felt suspicious about his motives.

Now I must confess at this point that I was not entirely blameless. I didn't make passes at his friends or even consider having an affair with anyone else when we were together. But these summer separations were another story. The previous summer I had had a relationship with a friend of a friend partly because I thought it likely Vittorio was doing the same in Italy. When he began to talk about his proposed trip for the coming summer, I told him about my affair the previous summer to try to dissuade him from going to Europe alone.

He was furious. He called me names and even hit me. It took him two days to finally come clean and admit that he wasn't being quite fair as he had had numerous relationships with other women since our marriage, telling me about each of them in some detail. His justification was that he wasn't harming me by having these affairs as long as he was fulfilling his conjugal duties as my husband. Whereas he said he had refrained from having any relationships in Italy because he knew I was being faithful to him at home. It was to me (given my Anglo-Saxon way of thinking) a very odd way of looking at the marital relationship, and one that was to cause more problems later on.

In fact, I think I could say that the problem was never really resolved. We did go to Europe together that summer, or at least he went and I followed. But we never seemed to stop arguing the whole summer. I think we were both trying to be as open and honest as possible. It was just that the more we talked, the less we seemed to understand one another and the more foreign the other's way of thinking seemed. Vittorio insisted that it was not the fact that I had had an affair that bothered him. No, that would be all right anytime. What bothered him, he said, was that I hadn't told him about it.

We somehow managed to get through the following school year and after that we again had to make other plans as there was no doctoral program at U.C. Santa Barbara. Vittorio chose five universities to apply to. He was refused by one (Berkeley) and accepted at the other four, three of which offered him fellowships. The two we finally had to choose between were the University of Washington at Seattle and the University of British Columbia in Vancouver.

There was another student in the Classics Department at Santa Barbara who had applied to many of the same universities and for whom the final decision came down to the same two. None of us had ever been in Canada, but I was already inclined toward making the move across the border for many of the same reasons that so many Americans were leaving the US in the late sixties and early seventies--the same reasons I had originally intended to remain in Europe. Vittorio, Jeff (the other student), and I went to the library at the university to see what we could find out about British Columbia, Vancouver in particular.

We researched the statistics about climate and population and talked to a library assistant who told us it was "beautiful". She said she had been in Vancouver for several days the year before and told us how great the scenery was. She said she had been told there were also fantastic mountains on the north shore but it had been too cloudy to see them the whole time she was there. We perused a Vancouver newspaper and were amazed at the low housing prices. We were baffled by some of the rental ads, however, as we couldn't figure out what the reference to "Kits" meant, not knowing that some twenty years later I would be living in "Kitsilano".

It didn't take any of us long to decide where we were going. First David had to be re-settled in the house in Carmel where he would be staying with the other children. Then Nicole and I would begin the long trip to Canada in our Volvo station wagon filled with some of our possessions. Vittorio and Jeff were to follow about a week later in a van packed with the rest.

Chapter X

Vittorio/Vancouver

In the two weeks between when I got to Vancouver with Nicole and when Vittorio and Jeff arrived with the van, I had managed to find a job for myself at Langara, the local community college, and had gotten us into student housing, neither of which had sounded possible from the inquiries we made before coming.

The job I found was tutoring in the "Gold Room", the college tutorial centre, a position that was shortly expanded to include teaching remedial writing classes. My background in crisis counseling plus the range of unusual teaching assignments I had had in California, from working with delinquent teen-aged girls in a group home and women inmates at the Santa Barbara County jail to teaching ex-convicts in Salinas, was an advantage. I had always known that it was the students I cared about more than any subject matter, and now I had my first chance, on an ongoing basis, to develop programs and teaching techniques specifically for students who might not otherwise be successful in college.

Nicole was registered in kindergarten at University Hill Elementary and was getting to know other children in Catania Circle, our small enclave in student housing.

The U.B.C. Classics Department was in transition when we arrived. A new department head, an American, was about to take over from the long-term, well-known previous one. The divisions in thought and interpretation we had observed in Santa Barbara were also obvious here except drawn along slightly different lines--the British and pro-British contingent versus everyone else. We were in the "everyone else" category along with the new department head. Though I don't feel Vittorio tried to isolate himself from other members of the department, he did develop a particularly good rapport with the new head that, again, put him clearly on one side of the division within the department. He was doing well with his classes, however, and was popular with the students assigned to him as part of the teaching requirement for his fellowship.

At home, as usual, there were many things happening with Vittorio that aroused my suspicions. There were letters from a woman in Santa Barbara whom I had never met but who seemed to know Vittorio quite well and was asking him to meet her where she was vacationing. Then there was the time he and a neighbor left a party together and didn't return so that eventually I had to go home on my own. Or the time I went over to the house of a person I considered my best friend to see why the coursework he was helping her with was taking so long.

I knocked several times. It was only a small student housing residence so they couldn't have failed to hear the knock. I walked away wondering if they had gone somewhere, waited, then walked back and tried again. This time they came to the door saying they were sorry, they simply had been so absorbed in the work they were doing they hadn't heard me. I wasn't convinced it was work they were so absorbed in.

Vittorio had always been pretty much a night person. Now he was able to control his schedule at school so that often he had no responsibilities before mid-afternoon. When I went to bed at night, usually before eleven as I had to work in the morning, he would either kiss me goodnight or come to bed with me for a while depending on what I wanted. After that he was presumably studying for the rest of the night. I'm sure part of that time was spent studying--it had to be. But more often than not, if I woke up in the middle of the night and went downstairs, he was nowhere around. Sometimes he had gone out and left the front door ajar. If our cat, Shyer, was also gone,

I felt some reassurance as I knew the cat often went for walks with him at night.

There were several rapes reported in student housing during that time. I even wondered if those could possibly be connected to Vittorio. I felt as if there was a dark side to his personality that I had had glimpses of and it frightened and confused me. How could I even think it possible that anyone so generally gentle and caring could be capable of such a thing? But I did wonder.

When I got home from work in the afternoons, Vittorio was often still in bed, just waking up and wanting me to fix him a coffee. Or else I arrived to find Nicole home from school and alone in the house. "Where's papa?" I asked her. She didn't know.

One night Vittorio came home not too late from spending some time at the university beer garden with other Classics Department students. We were lying in bed together listening to music and making love. Vittorio said it really wasn't much different from having sex with a virgin. I asked him what he meant. He said he had just come from having sex with one of the younger students in the department.

I went into a state of something between shock and disbelief. I wanted not to have heard what he had just told me.

And I stayed in that state for the weeks that followed. We talked about it, of course. I insisted that he have no further contact with her, but he continued to see her saying he couldn't let her down, that "she needed him and he felt sorry for her". I couldn't seem to make him see that his first obligation was to me, his wife, whom he had hurt greatly by his behavior, rather than to a young student to whom he really owed nothing, no matter how sorry he might feel for her.

One afternoon we were at a Classics Department party at a fellow student's house when the young woman in question arrived and sat down at a nearby table. I was feeling extremely uncomfortable and even more annoyed because one of the faculty members seemed to find the situation vastly amusing. I finally couldn't tolerate just sitting there doing nothing any longer. I stood up and asked the girl to follow me. We walked to a park about a block away with Vittorio following at a discrete distance--I think he was afraid of what I might do to her.

We sat down on a log half facing each other. I asked her "why?" How could she have done something she must have known would be so hurtful to someone else? She responded that it was the first time a man had paid any particular attention to her and that she had been flattered and therefore just couldn't say "no". I don't remember the rest of the conversation though I know it was brief. I had my answer, and for me it was no answer at all. It didn't help to know what her reasons were. And it helped even less that neither of them seemed willing to apologize or indeed to give up what they had started.

I had friends, of course, who said they couldn't see why I was so upset. Why should I care so much about my husband's having a brief fling with a not very attractive student he insisted he only felt sorry for. He said all along he was not in love with her and certainly there was no mention of his leaving me for her. He wanted me to see it as just an adventure on his part, one of those things he felt it was important for him to experience in life (another one he had yet to experience, he mentioned, was having sex with a nun). He even suggested that perhaps I would be reassured if he brought her over to the house so the three of us could have sex together.

After three weeks or so of talking, arguing, tears on my part and stomping out of the house and slamming the door on his, I had had enough. I was barely able to function in the classroom or to keep up any normal routine at home for Nicole's sake.

Finally my classes were over for the year. I waited until Vittorio was out of the house, packed some clothes for myself and Nicole and, telling only my "best friend" where I was going, picked Nicole up at school and headed for Harrison Hot Springs, a lake resort about an hour and a half outside Vancouver.

It felt good to get away from all the tension I had been surrounded by at home and to relax in the hot pools. We had been there only about two days, however, when Vittorio arrived, my "friend" having told him where I was. He showed up with a bouquet of roses in one hand and a bottle of champagne in the other and literally begged me to come back swearing nothing of that sort would ever happen again. How could anyone refuse his display of devotion, at once funny, ardent, and pathetic. Once again, I gave in.

The rest of the summer, though, I remember being haunted by the image of that girl. If we went to a concert, she was sure to have a seat just a few rows away. At the folk festival that summer I remember being stretched out on the grass on our blanket enjoying the evening's music only to turn and find her sitting on an adjacent blanket. It ruined the rest of the evening for me, but neither she nor Vittorio said anything or showed any signs of recognizing each other. It almost seemed to me like some sort of game Vittorio was playing.

I've often wondered why I was really so upset. "Yes, of course", some people will say, "Naturally you were hurt! How could you not have been?" But others, more often than not those with faithful spouses who have never strayed, will say, "Come on! After all, was it really worth getting that disturbed about?"

In fact, I can see the rationale for accepting the situation. But "rationale" is the key word here. What the mind may be able to accept, the emotions often cannot. And what I was reacting to was not simply a betrayal on Vittorio's part toward me. It went much deeper. My whole self concept, self esteem, whatever you want to call it, seemed crushed by his actions. It was the ultimate rejection of every tenuous edifice of self-confidence I had so carefully constructed over many years of work and effort. I simply ceased to be able to function. It was, at least in part, my father's emotional rejection of me all over again. Realizing that was one thing. Doing something to change it was quite another.

For the next year or so, Vittorio and I shared the same house, more or less. He moved out for a while, into a neighbor's basement. But mostly he slept on a single cot in our basement surrounded by his winemaking equipment and the shelved bottles of Zinfandel and Ruby Cabernet he had made with equipment borrowed from Italian wine producers on Commercial Drive.

He was running around with a very young crowd, some hardly out of high school. He had decided to teach himself to play guitar, and he and his friends could often be heard late at night singing Bob Dylan songs in the basement. There was one young man in particular that he seemed to be spending a lot of time with. One night I came home from seeing a film with a friend and found the two of them sitting together on the couch drinking wine. They had both had more than enough, but Vittorio insisted on leaving with the young man saying they were going out to the liquor store for more wine, what for I don't know as we had a good supply in the basement.

I went to bed a short time later but was awakened by a phone call about two that morning. It was Vittorio calling from the police station and pretending not to speak English because apparently he had told the police officer who arrested him that he didn't understand English. He was being held and charged with "refusing to blow" because he wouldn't take a Breathalyzer test.

When he eventually appeared in court, with one of our neighbors who happened to be a lawyer representing him, the charge had been changed to "obstructing justice" since after they finally succeeded in getting a breath sample from him, he pulled the plug on the equipment as soon as they left the room. With me, our neighbor the lawyer, and Vittorio's young friend all present, he was given a fine of $300 and a suspended sentence.

By this time Vittorio had finished his course work at the university. He was negotiating the topic for his dissertation with the doctoral committee. He had chosen a topic based on an interpretation of one of Euripides' plays. The committee turned down his proposal. They said it was because something too similar to it had already been done. I suspect it had more to do with that old split in ways of interpreting Greek comedies. They simply didn't agree with Vittorio's interpretation.

He didn't argue with them. They had suggested an alternative topic to him and he tried to research it. But it just wasn't something he could get enthusiastic about. It was their topic, not his.

Things had been dragging on this way for some time when Vittorio got a letter from a friend who had gone to Japan a few months earlier to teach English. The friend was telling him how easy it was to get jobs there and how much money he could make. He could even set things up for Vittorio at the same school where he was teaching.

It was a tempting offer given the bogged down state of his studies and our relationship. We both knew that if he quit his program then, it was unlikely he would ever finish, and that with anything less than a doctorate in Classics, he had no chance of teaching in that field. Nevertheless, going to Japan would be, for Vittorio, a respite from what seemed more and more like a stalemate in the Classics department. It would also be a chance for the two of us to be apart long enough to think about whether we wanted to continue our marriage.

Before Vittorio left for Japan, we agreed that it made sense not to make any promises of sexual fidelity to each other since we were likely to be separated for many months. Vittorio also repeated what he had said before, that he was not concerned about my having a relationship with someone else but that he wanted to be told about it. That statement was soon put to the test.

Not long after he left I became involved with someone who was staying with a friend in student housing. It was a brief affair, only a matter of weeks, but refreshing to be with someone totally unlike Vittorio, someone familiarly North American. I wrote and told Vittorio about it. In his answering letter he tried to remain non-committal, but I was sure I was not wrong in sensing a suppressed anger and frustration that he hardly dared show. I felt a definite sense of satisfaction, call it revenge if you like.

Shortly after that brief affair was over and the person in question had left town, I became involved with the friend he'd been staying with. Again it lasted only a matter of weeks as we both knew it was inappropriate, age difference being part of the reason. I had already been twelve years older than Vittorio. I was some seventeen years older than this man. He went on to other girlfriends, but I remained his friend and confidante, as I have to this day.

Vittorio was also informed about this second lover and his response was the same. Shortly after that, however, Vittorio came back for a visit and I had a chance to introduce the two of them. Vittorio was doing his best to remain nonchalant, but the emotional agitation was clearly visible in his actions and tone of voice. Again, I must admit enjoying his discomfort.

The first Christmas Vittorio was in Japan we met in Hawaii for two weeks during the holiday. It was an amicable two weeks as both of us wanted to enjoy our holiday without arguing about anything. Since one of the passions we shared was swimming, especially in clear warm water, having a pleasant holiday was not too difficult. We went to one beach in the morning, another in the afternoon, and often still another in the evening. All this swimming plus a bit of snorkeling and some body surfing also suited Nicole just fine as she takes after both of us in that respect.

It almost seemed at the end of our holiday as if it might be possible to salvage our marriage. It was to that end that I agreed to go to Japan with Nicole the following summer, just for a visit, to see what it was like and explore the possibility of moving there. However Vittorio had one more trip to make back to Canada before that.

For reasons I didn't understand at the time, he chose to fly into Seattle instead of Vancouver and have me pick him up at the airport there. When we crossed the border, he made sure I was driving as customs and immigration officials rarely question me whereas he is always stopped and questioned. I simply smiled and said I lived in Vancouver and had just picked up my husband at the airport, and we were waved across.

It was probably the next day that Vittorio showed me the passport he had been traveling on. He still had an Italian passport as he had only had permanent residence status in the

U.S. and had lost that by coming to Canada. He had been on a student visa in Canada until I was able to sponsor him by applying for landed immigrant status in Canada as head of the family on the basis of my job at Langara.

The problem was that his Italian passport had expired. He had altered it so that it appeared to be current, but he knew it wouldn't pass close scrutiny. So shortly after returning to Canada, he destroyed the passport and then reported it missing to the R.C.M.P. He wanted me to come in with him while he filed the report but I refused. His next step was to apply for Canadian citizenship, something I had done for myself and Nicole awhile earlier. He conveniently forgot to tell them, of course, about his residency status because he couldn't legally apply while living in Japan.

A few days later, two of his students arrived from Japan. Nicole and I were staying temporarily in the basement suite of a friend who owned a large house and rented out bedrooms. She happened to have several vacancies at the time and said she could also accommodate Vittorio's students.

When the students arrived at the airport, one of them was retained a short time in customs. Vittorio seemed overly anxious and solicitous when she emerged. Later that evening after the girls had been shown their respective rooms, Vittorio and I took them with us to the house of some friends with whom we had planned to spend the evening. I felt a little uncomfortable at the way this particular girl sat on the floor next to Vittorio's chair and the way he kept inquiring if she was all right. "Was she warm enough?" "Was she catching a cold?" But no one else seemed to notice. Or if they did, they didn't say anything.

We went back fairly early in the evening to my friend's house where we were staying, and I went to bed, assuming Vittorio would follow shortly. I woke up in the middle of the night--it must have been two or three--and wondered where Vittorio was. I went upstairs to the main floor of the house. There were lights on in the kitchen and family room area, but no one seemed to be around. Then, as I walked through the dining room, some movement in the living room across the hall caught my attention.

The living room was a formal room used by the owner only for special occasions, so I wasn't expecting to see anyone in there. But as I went closer, I could see through the partly ajar glass doors some movement on the rug in front of the sofa. As I drew closer, I saw in the light reflected from the other room Vittorio standing up hurriedly pulling up his pants and some movement on the rug beneath where he had been. I didn't need to go farther to know what was happening.

I stepped into the dining room and waited until, a few minutes later, they emerged, Vittorio with the Japanese student following behind. I told them both to get out of the house, "NOW"! Vittorio instructed the student to go to her room saying I should go back to bed, that "it was nothing; they were just friends and were just fooling around". I repeated my demand that he and the student leave the house immediately, but he refused to take me seriously. Eventually I had to phone a friend to come and get him and the student out of the house.

That was it. I contacted a lawyer and filed for divorce the next day. Vittorio once again pleaded with me to reconsider, but this time I had really had enough. When he saw that I was not going to be dissuaded from filing for divorce, he decided to counter sue although he had already returned to Japan by that time, thus making it an even more time-consuming and expensive process.

Two things that came out of the divorce proceedings were unexpected. First, my lawyer, a woman, asked me whether there had been any inappropriate behavior on Vittorio's part toward my children. I told her about the incident years before involving Bekah. She suggested that I ask Nicole if Vittorio had ever approached her in any way that made her feel uncomfortable. I did, and saw that Nicole was upset by the question though her answer seemed innocuous enough, that sometimes when I wasn't home from work yet and Vittorio was still in bed he would pull her over and try to kiss her and that when she tried to pull away he would say, "What's the matter? Don't you like that? Mama does."

The second surprise was Vittorio's asking for a piece of property in California we had bought jointly, though the money had come from a mortgage on my mother's house. He had always, as a true communist--though he now declared himself an anarchist--decried individual ownership of property. He had said he thought communal living was best, that even cooking should be done communally with everyone taking turns preparing meals. Of course, he never did any of the preparing at home.

At any rate, given current divorce laws in Canada, I was told I was lucky to get off with his asking for only one piece of property as there were others including my mother's house in Palo Alto. I finally agreed on the terms that the property remain in both our names as long as Nicole was still a minor or remained a student and until he had fulfilled his commitment to child support.

It was a good plan. With Vittorio in Japan, I would have had no way of collecting child support without his legal claim to the property depending on his fulfilling his duty to Nicole.

Vittorio has remained in Japan ever since and eventually married the Japanese girl in question though he made a point of phoning to tell me when he got married that it was not for love. He said he needed "someone to take care of him in his old age".

I wonder how many generations of Japanese students are now roaming the world speaking English with an Italian accent. Somehow over the years he has managed to pass himself off as an American even to the point of changing his name to "Victor", but his accent must be obvious to native speakers of English.

Still, he manages to keep working, even though he has changed jobs several times. His situation there seems quite tenuous as younger native speakers would certainly have preference over him for the available jobs. And when he can no longer work--what then? He can never be a Japanese citizen and has no pension rights there. He could come back to Canada, but what would he do here? He could return to Italy but to what?

It was for these reasons that a couple of years ago, when Nicole had finally decided she had had enough of school, on one of my yearly trips to California to see my older children, I went to the Land Title office in Salinas and signed the California property over to him. He had been prompt and regular about his child support payments and generous to Nicole on birthdays and Christmas.

I had long since forgiven him for any hurt he had caused me because I knew something about what he had been through as a child. I could even excuse an incident that had happened years before when Nicole had visited him in Japan. As I understood it, he had come home drunk one night, crawled into bed with Nicole and tried to have sexual relations with her. I could manage to excuse that only because I saw it as a one-time occurrence and something he had done when drunk. In the last few years, though, I have gradually been made aware that that was not the only time. It had started much earlier when we were still living together.

I can understand those who would say, "Stupid woman!" "How could she not have seen what was going on?" "How could she fail to protect her daughter?" And even worse, once knowing about even one incident, "How could she ever forgive that man?" In fact why not immediately take him to court and charge him with sexual abuse?

Aside from the fact that his being in Japan would make a case against him extremely difficult to pursue, I suppose the reason for not pursuing any legal remedy is partly that the knowledge of what really happened has only been gradually disclosed over time and partly the realization that the issues here are not all that simple.

I've finally reached a point where I no longer have any communication with Vittorio. I've even stopped writing the casual thank-you notes for money sent to Nicole--a responsibility I took on several years ago when she felt she no longer wanted to communicate with him.

If I let myself dwell on the effect of his actions on Nicole and how the impact of his behavior may be responsible for the lack of self-confidence that has interfered with her successfully completing a school program or going ahead in job--related activities, I get so angry I can visualize myself firing a gun at Vittorio at point blank range. It is only within my range of capabilities to forgive what he has done to me personally. At some point Nicole must decide for herself when and to what extent she is able to forgive.

I also know that nothing is quite that simply good or bad, black or white. Vittorio, to this day, will not admit to any responsibility for what he has done. But then neither will he discuss his mother's death. Nor will he face the traumas he experienced as a child. So who is really to blame and for what? There is no one way of looking at anything. In some societies incest is acceptable. In many, a man having one or even several relations with women other than his wife is the norm.

When Vittorio and I divorced, about half of my friends said to me, "It's about time you left that jerk". But there were an equal number who were silent and avoided me thereafter, signifying, I thought, that they were more in sympathy with Vittorio. I can understand that. Vittorio is a very complex person--a brilliant scholar equally at home building a house or tending a garden and whose interests range from study of languages (he knew about eight at last count) to transcribing words to Bob Dylan's songs. He also had a very dark side, one that has hurt others, but in the long run, no one more than himself.

Sometimes out of great darkness and difficulty come enlightenment and beauty. I could see the potential for enlightenment and beauty in Vittorio, which is why I stayed with him so long and why, although I abhor so much of his behavior, I am reluctant to condemn him as a person.

During our years together it always struck me as strange the amount of "bad luck" Vittorio could attract to himself for no apparent reason. If we went out to dinner, the restaurant he wanted to eat at would invariably be closed. Or if it were open, they were sure to be out of the item he wanted on the menu. Any kind of day-to-day business was always more complicated for him. He simply couldn't get the right person on the phone at the right time to accomplish anything, something I never seemed to have any trouble with.

And as for cars! For me, having driven so many years without an accident, I couldn't understand Vittorio's record of several accidents per year. It was certainly not a lack of coordination or inability to drive! He just always seemed to be walking under a black cloud. Perhaps that explains why his favorite comic book character was Charlie Brown.

The more I think about it, the more I'm convinced that "bad luck" isn't luck at all but rather a subconscious self-destructive impulse. Is it possible that underneath Vittorio's cheerful, outgoing demeanor was some sort of self loathing that caused him to wreak havoc on those around him, especially those he was closest to, thus guaranteeing the negation of any possible happiness or productive life?

I don't have the answers. I only know that whatever anger I feel is tempered with sadness, sadness that someone with so much potential should be afflicted by so deep a darkness, not entirely of his own making.

Chapter XI

Mother

During the trip down I kept thinking of the movie "Thelma and Louise". Though aside from the fact that it was two women in a car making a trip, there wasn't much similarity. I was showing my friend Lee the Oregon and California coast I was familiar with from driving that route numerous times before, and we were stopping in hostels--which was new to Lee. But although we were exploring restaurants and shops and checking out hostels, many of the interesting stops along the way had to be by-passed with an agreement that we would stop there again on the way back or "some other time". After all we did have a sort of deadline--pardon the pun.

We had left Saturday morning and had promised the hospital we would arrive in Palo Alto by Monday afternoon to pick up my mother--well not really to pick up, rather to "make arrangements" as I believe it is euphemistically called, because by the time I had organized the trip to visit my mother in the hospital and was ready to leave Vancouver Saturday morning, I already knew from talking to my daughter in Monterey that my mother was dead.

On the way down I kept wondering, with almost scientific curiosity, what I felt. I had always wondered what I would feel when my mother died. One makes certain assumptions about the feelings a child must have for his or her mother. But I knew that my feelings didn't fit any of those assumptions.

I decided I didn't feel much of anything about her death. I had felt a certain revulsion for her physical untidiness that got progressively worse as she got older and an irritation at her self-centeredness and continual demands on me mixed with a sense of sadness that anyone's life, not just hers, had to come down to this sort of totally dependent state. I paid her bills, bought pajamas and blouses and deodorant and address books and sent money every month. But I lied.

I lied because I never told her that I really didn't love her. In fact when pressed to it by certain circumstances such as the rare occasion when she, at the end of a telephone conversation, might say briefly "I love you", I would respond almost mechanically, "I love you too." But it was a lie. I've never loved her. But what was the point in telling the truth. What would have been the purpose, either for her or me? One only tells a hard, terrible truth like that when there is something to be gained from it, when after the shock and hurt there is the possibility of a reconciliation, of a real love and bonding.

Bekah, my daughter in Monterey, has always been good at that sort of free expression of feelings--positive or negative. She is often so open with her feelings that I feel my personal space intruded upon. Her father, who is considerably more reserved than I am, finds her frankness profoundly disturbing. But she was the one, toward the end, when my mother was in the hospital, who was able to give her the unconditional love she needed and which I was unable to give.

Even if I had been there, which I wasn't, I don't think I would have been able to bridge the distance between us. I have been with rather casual friends near death and felt an amazing closeness to them. But sometimes it is easier to feel closeness with a casual acquaintance or even a stranger than blood kin. Perhaps that emotional distance between two people so closely related by blood is uncomfortable because of what we feel should be there or because of what unknown emotion we think may be hiding behind that apparent lack of feeling.

Anyway I kept wondering, on the way down, what I actually felt. I wasn't at all obsessed or preoccupied by my mother's death. In fact most of the time I even forgot, in the process of deciding when to get gas or where to stop for lunch or how to get the temperature in the car just right, what our real purpose was in being on the road at all.

It was more that when we had to bypass a particularly pleasant hiking trail or set of rustic shops, I would remember that the hospital had kindly agreed to hold my mother for me until we got there. And although thoughts passed through my mind almost randomly, like clouds in a sky--thoughts about warm weather and its effect on body conditions--they had assured me that there was no rush, relatives often could not arrive for several days. So I assumed they had "facilities" for these circumstances, that is some sort of refrigerated area-- which finally in these shorthand cloud-thoughts became "Mother on ice" which of course brought all sorts of other connotations such as "'Stars on Ice". And the more unserious and slightly disrespectful the images became, the funnier they seemed, and the funnier, of course, the more inappropriate to the situation. And the more inappropriate, the funnier.

The first day was an easy drive. We didn't get out of Vancouver until almost eleven and reached Portland by six, in time for a leisurely stroll and a meal at a gourmet restaurant near the hostel.

The second day Lee and I drove from Portland all the way to the hostel at Leggett at the southern end of the California Redwoods. It was our longest day of driving. We had stopped for groceries in Eureka and then again for some sightseeing at the little coastal village of Trinidad, so it had been dark for over an hour when we finally pulled into the driveway of the hostel. I had been to this particular hostel several times before and wanted to show Lee the sandy beach and deep river swimming hole. But it was dark and we were both tired and still hadn't had any dinner.

The hostel was more crowded than when I had been there before. There was the usual assortment of young travelers from various countries--Israel, Finland, New Zealand--and a family from somewhere in the southern U.S. with seven children ranging in age from around nine to about two months.

We chatted with the people preparing meals in the kitchen, borrowing this knife, that pan, cutting board, etc. and finally had our veggies ready to sauté, our rice on to boil, and a small salad prepared. By the time we were ready to eat, it was almost ten and the children had been shuffled off to bed. So we were able to make room at one of the tables--the one they weren't using for a game of Scrabble.

After dinner, Lee and I stretched out in the overstuffed chairs in the living room area to relax and drink a cup of tea. I don't remember exactly how it came up, but I suppose it was one of those moments when one takes stock of just where one is, what has been accomplished, and what remains to be done. We had gotten two thirds of the way to our destination and calculated we could be at the hospital by about two the following afternoon.

The images of my mother waiting for us "on ice" came back to me along with the old urban legend about the family traveling in a foreign country with their dead granny rolled in a blanket on the top of the car and having the car stolen with granny still on it. I decided Lee was a good enough friend that my bizarre thoughts wouldn't shock her or seem truly disrespectful. But as I shared some of my fairly stream-of-consciousness thoughts, I started laughing and so did Lee. And the more we laughed, the more bizarre thoughts came to mind and the more we couldn't stop laughing until I'm sure the Scrabble players at the table behind us thought we were quite strange. I wonder if they caught or understood any part of our cryptic conversation and, if so, what they made of it or what they thought we were laughing at.

But somehow the more I imagined their interpretation of overheard bits of our conversation --which included exploring different denotations and connotations of the word "mother" such as being a substance that forms in a bottle and the Black English "motha"--the more absurd the whole situation of Lee and I being there on route to our particular errand seemed to be and the more uncontrollable we were.

Finally, having exhausted our linguistic explorations and ourselves and it being lights-out time for the hostel, we trotted out to our cabin and got settled in our wool blanket-covered sleeping sacs.

The next morning we were off again. We reached Sausalito in time for a late lunch and then phoned to tell the people at the hospital we would be there soon. Actually we were in Sausalito longer than we expected and didn't reach the hospital until almost four.

I had been told, when I phoned the hospital before leaving Vancouver, to come to the front desk when I arrived and tell them that my mother had died there the previous Saturday and that I was there to "make arrangements". I understood that there would be a social worker available to advise me about morticians' services.

I was tired and a bit lightheaded from the three days of driving but figured the hardest part was over. All I had to do now was let them know I was there and a kindly social worker would help me through the rest. I had already decided that unless there were instructions from my mother to the contrary, I would opt for cremation. That seemed to be the simplest, cleanest, and probably most inexpensive option. My mother's parents had been both been cremated, and I felt that it would be my choice for myself. I was less sure what should be done with the ashes afterward or whether or what kind of memorial service there should be.

My mother had lived in Palo Alto most of her life. But the majority of her friends were gone. The contacts she had left seemed to consist of a bible group who visited her fairly regularly at the long term care facility and a few of her previous drinking buddies from the old days when she could still manage to smuggle a bottle or two of vodka into the place where she was living.

I wanted nothing to do with either group. My limited dealings with them had consisted mostly of telephone conversations in which they either listed all the things my mother wanted me to send her or requests for money to cover "expenses" for my mother--"expenses" that had somehow caused several thousand dollars to disappear from her bank account in less than six months.

So here I was, standing at the front reception desk at Stanford University Hospital telling the main receptionist that I had arrived and was ready to "make arrangements" for my mother.

She motioned to me, and to Lee who was standing nearby, to take a seat on a line of chairs near the desk where there was a family group including a fussy baby being alternately comforted by mother and grandmother. We sat down and waited. After a few minutes, a young, neatly dressed woman with a paper-filled folder appeared from behind the main desk and asked us what we wanted. I explained again that my mother had died and that I had driven down from Vancouver to make arrangements for her.

She shuffled through some papers in the folder and then said that the arrangements had already been made by phone and the Chaplain's office had signed for me. She seemed to be saying that she didn't see why I was there. I tried to explain that, in fact, no arrangements were yet made because I still needed to find someone to do the cremation and that, since I lived out of town, I had come down expecting to be given some advice on the matter. She seemed impatient and strode off saying she would contact the Chaplain's office.

So much for my expectations of being given a warm and sympathetic welcome by a helpful social worker!

By the time the Chaplain arrived some minutes later, Lee had gone off to make a phone call, and I found myself suddenly in tears. It occurred to me, even as it was happening, that my tears were a bit deceitful in that the people behind the desk, and the Chaplain when he arrived, probably thought my tears were a response to losing my mother whereas I knew that they were simply the result of the tension and frustration of being treated so cavalierly after such a long trip--much as one may break into tears at a foreign airport as a result of not being able to find a cab.

The Chaplain, when he arrived, tried to be comforting but, of course, not knowing the reason for the tears, and not having access to the information I needed, he wasn't able to do much.

When Lee returned from her phone call, we tried to make it clear to the people at the desk that it was a social worker we needed to talk to, and they told us they would page her. We waited for at least another twenty minutes--we had already been there almost an hour--and when they told us for the second or third time that she still had not responded, I decided I had had enough. If they had been able to keep my mother for me this long they could keep her one more day! I went back to the desk and told them we were leaving and would come back in the morning.

As it turned out, leaving at that point was the best decision we could have made. After spending the night at a peaceful, tree-studded hostel in the Los Altos hills, I was in a much better state of mind to cope with all the intricacies of the arrangements that needed to be made. It also helped that the social worker arrived promptly at the information desk and was able to take us to her private office to discuss options instead of having to deal with them in the publicity and confusion of the area surrounding the front desk.

We compared prices for cremation and memorial services of several mortuaries in the area, spoke to a couple of their representatives on the phone, and finally settled on a company in Burlingame. They would arrange to pick up my mother at the hospital, do a simple cremation for $450, take care of providing the death certificate, and have the "cremains" neatly packaged for me to pick up in a few days. I could decide what I wanted to do about a memorial service and what to do with the "cremains" later.

I was relieved when it was over, not only that the "arrangements" had been made but also that no one had suggested to me that I might want to see my mother one last time. I didn't. Fortunately this was California where the cultural tendency is to pretend insofar as possible that death doesn't exist, so I wasn't asked to perform any of the rituals that would have been expected in another time or place.

With everything taken care of, Lee and I drove the short distance to the Stanford shopping center and had lunch on an outdoor patio. The sun was pleasantly warm and the odors of flowers in nearby planters mixed with the smells of various foods being eaten at surrounding tables. Birds hopped brazenly onto tables recently deserted to retrieve leftover crumbs.

It felt good to have basically accomplished our mission. All we had on the agenda now was to go on down to Carmel, stay with my daughter Bekah for a few days, which would give me a chance to show Lee around the Monterey Peninsula. And then, by Thursday, we would be on our way back to Canada after picking up my mother's ashes in Burlingame.

When we finished lunch, a few things remained to be done, such as collecting my mother's belongings at the care centre. They had placed everything in plastic bags and the bags on top of her stripped bed. I went through the contents quickly, taking out only things like photographs and other personal items. Lee helped me take down from the wall the drawings done by my granddaughter, Ashley, that I had put up on my last visit. We straightened out the finances in the manager's office and collected an envelope with a cheque in it that I had sent from Vancouver the previous week and that had just arrived there that morning.

Since we had a little time to spare, I drove Lee around Palo Alto--down the palm tree-lined boulevard from the university, under the railroad underpass to the main street of a renovated downtown area complete with wall murals, block-sized corner parks with fountains and hanging baskets and adjacent natural foods restaurants, and farther along the same street, the stately homes of those who had been there when the town and the university were new.

We stopped a few blocks away at the house, now renovated and turned into professional offices that had been my mother's home when she was a girl. It wasn't one of the colonial style mansions of University Boulevard, but a large Victorian corner house, apparently considered architecturally worthy enough by the city council to have been designated a heritage building, with a plaque in front commemorating its history.

We also drove past the place I had lived from first grade until I moved to San Jose in my second year of college. The small peach-colored stucco bungalow with its fake row of Spanish tiles at the front was no longer there. The people I had sold it to several years before were still in the process of building. But I could show Lee the neighborhood with its park, community centre, adult and children's theater, Scout House, elementary school, playground, tennis courts, and especially the swimming pool where I had spent so much of my time every summer.

We stayed at the hostel one more night, then headed for Monterey where I was hoping to show Lee some of the local points of interest. The problem was that Lee had only been free to take this trip with me at the last moment because the union at U.B.C., where she worked, was on strike. She was keeping in touch by phone with various people who knew how the negotiations were going, and the night before we started for Monterey, which, for her, was to be the most interesting part of the trip, her sources were informing her that a meeting to be held shortly might resolve the dispute.

By the time we got to Monterey, she had decided she had no choice but to catch a flight back to Vancouver that evening.

So I tried to cram a grand tour of the Monterey Peninsula into about three hours that afternoon. By five we were at Bekah's apartment where Roy, her boyfriend, was already home from work, and by 5:30 were on our way to the airport--before Bekah had even arrived to meet Lee.

After visiting with my family for a few days and conferring with them about whether we wanted a memorial service, it was clear that no one had any particular need or enthusiasm for one. So all that remained to be done was to pick up my mother's ashes in Burlingame and start home to Vancouver, deciding on the way what to do with them. I briefly considered placing them in the cemetery in Palo Alto since my mother's brother Morris and his wife Irene were buried there, but when I saw their cozy grave together I knew that the only option the cemetery managers were offering me, to place my mother in the same grave with them, wasn't feasible--especially since they hadn't spoken to her in over forty years.

I stopped on the way back to Vancouver at a place in the Redwoods where I had been several times on other trips. It was a bend in the river with a path through the trees leading to a sandy beach. I remembered visiting the Redwoods with my mother and stepfather as a child and thought my mother might like her ashes scattered there.

The problem was that the box I had been given containing the ashes was labeled with a warning of the illegality of distributing ashes in the state of California. I tried to be discreet, waiting until all other visiting cars were gone from the parking area and keeping the box containing the ashes in an unmarked paper bag.

I walked down one of the pathways parallel to the river until I found a spot in the trees overlooking the beach. I couldn't go farther into the bush because I was surrounded by poison oak, and with my extreme sensitivity to poison oak, I didn't dare go off the path. I saw no one around. So I took the inner hard plastic box out of its cardboard container and tried to open it. But I couldn't see any way of getting it open without a can opener or a sharp knife. "Well", I thought, "so this is how they are going to prevent me from breaking California law!" Since I was on a public path and didn't seem to be making any progress with the box, I soon gave up and headed back to the car.

No other likely places presented themselves. So when I arrived in Vancouver, the bag, box, and contents were still in the back of my station wagon and stayed there for several days as I had more important things to cart up the elevator to my fourth floor apartment.

When I did finally go down to get the ashes (not having decided yet what to do with them), I reached the door to the elevator at about the same time as a couple from the third floor who hadn't seen me since my return. They asked how my trip had been and how my mother was, since the last they had heard she was in the hospital. I said my trip had been fine but that my mother was dead, and feeling at that moment the weight of the box I was holding was tempted to add, continuing in my cheery tone of voice, "In fact, here she is." But I thought it might strike them as too macabre, and let the moment pass.

A few days later, while walking in my favorite park nearby, I decided I had found the perfect place. It was an open meadow with a circle of stones that served as a fire pit. I had heard that it was considered a sacred spot to Native people. In fact, I had seen there on several occasions what appeared to be small Native gatherings or ceremonies.

There was a backdrop of trees and blackberry bushes and a trail leading up a hill behind the fire pit, while, looking in the other direction across the meadow, there was a view over a pond to the grassy hillside of the park and beyond that, the waters of Burrard Inlet and the North Shore mountains. I had always had a special fondness for this park and, whether imagined or not, had always seemed to feel a spiritual presence in the meadow. I thought maybe the Native spirits there wouldn't mind if I brought my mother to join them. So I asked my youngest daughter, Nicole, to help me scatter the ashes.

There were some other people at the fire pit when we arrived, so we started up the hill, scattering some of the ashes where they would fertilize the roots of the blackberry bushes. Then, when the fire pit area was vacant, we took the rest of the ashes and stirred them in with the ashes of the pit. I had brought along a copy of the 23rd Psalm to read. I needed to have it in writing because I wasn't sure I could remember all of it otherwise. I explained to Nicole that I had chosen it because Grandmother Kirksey had taught it to me when I was a child, and it had always been a special prayer for me for that reason.

We read the prayer and then just sat quietly on the logs surrounding the fire pit. It was a little hard to have much of a service as I've always tried to protect my children from the over zealousness of most religions. But I felt comfortable with what we had done and felt that I had chosen the right place.

Even though my mother had never visited Canada when she was alive, I was glad I had finally brought her here to rest. We had not been close, and my relationship with her had become more and more difficult over the years. But now that she was dead, my image of her as an angry, petty, selfish old woman seemed to fade, and instead I saw her in my mind's eye as the lithe, graceful twenty-something young woman from the family albums I had sorted through and organized for my oldest son the previous Christmas.

*****

I walk in the park almost every day and nearly always make a detour in the path so as to stop by the fire pit. It's funny though. I chose the fire pit because it was a sacred place. My only reservation had been whether I had been committing some sort of sacrilege putting my mother's ashes there. When Nicole remarked as we walked away that day that it was obviously a place where kids hung out at night to drink, it came as a bit of a surprise. Not that I hadn't seen the bottles and cigarette wrappers, but somehow it just hadn't registered. For a minute I wondered if I'd chosen the wrong place but then realized it was just where she would feel most at home--I had provided her with what she always liked best--some lively drinking companions.

Chapter XII

Jericho

He maketh me to lie down in green pastures.
He leadeth me beside the still waters.
He restoreth my soul.
23rd Psalm

I walk at Jericho nearly every day, sometimes twice a day in the summer. I like to go early in the morning before it gets crowded or in the evening after dinner, sometime around sunset.

Most of the people at Jericho walk along the main path that follows the beachfront. My favorite places to walk are either on the beach itself, right at the water's edge where I can hear and feel the rhythm of the waves, or else along the edge of the ponds where I can observe the ducks and coots, Canada Geese in season, or catch a glimpse of a Blue Heron standing resolutely still among the reeds.

I like walking through the places where the forest converges on the path and shades it on a hot day, though I am always more wary there knowing the possible dangers, especially for women, in a city park. There are certain points along my walk where I know the rabbits live under the tangles of blackberry bushes and I watch to see what colors of rabbits will appear and whether, especially in spring, there will be baby rabbits.

In spring I look forward to seeing the first baby ducks and then watching from day to day as they grow bigger. They learn very quickly that people often have crumbs for them and will trip over themselves to reach any pair of feet pausing near the water's edge. Meanwhile mother duck, who also knows about the handouts, but is more cautious, quacks at them from a short distance away.

The other day I found myself surrounded by half a dozen ducklings. I told them I had nothing for them and started to walk away. They persisted in following me and were soon joined by several more. I ended up being followed by some dozen or more ducklings half way around the pond, their mothers voicing disapproval all the way, much to the amusement of other visitors to the park that day.

The other place I often stop is the circle of stones in the meadow behind the ponds. It took me awhile to recognize that the seemingly random stones around the fire pit were not random after all, that they formed a medicine wheel or sacred circle. I still don't know much about it, but enough to know that if I enter, it is best to enter from the south and that I must ask permission of the spirits there. I know I should be purified by smudging first and should request permission from an elder. But I always ask the spirits' permission to enter with genuine respect, and I hope that is enough.

I have had a lot of time to think in the last few years, especially on these walks. I can look at my life in some perspective now that I am removed from the emotional entanglement of intimate relationships or the day-to-day struggle to earn a living. It is a pleasant plateau to have arrived at, more objective, more serene than the sometimes-chaotic existence I for so long accepted as "normal".

One of the things I realize now is that there are multiple ways to see any given experience. When I now look back, I feel relatively satisfied with what my life has been. But I can easily see that from another perspective it could be considered a failure. I also see how certain circumstances of my infancy and early childhood caused me to take certain paths and make certain decisions.

Because part of the time before I was six was spent with a grandmother who gave me love and security, there is a part of me that feels loved and secure, and whenever my surroundings and the people I am relating to allow it, that feeling of love, security, and being at home in the world comes to the forefront. When I encounter people who react negatively toward me or when I am in a stressful or difficult situation, however, all the insecurity of the child left alone in the convent or positioned as the outsider with her father's family comes back to haunt me.

I also know now why I was attracted to certain relationships and made the career choices I did. I never felt quite comfortable with "happy", "normal" people. Something was always missing when I visited friends who had parents who stayed together and related to each other and their children without dysfunctional behavior patterns. I wanted to be part of such families but always felt alienated from them. Whereas when I was with a person or family where there were clearly problems, where things were not quite working, I felt at home. And if I thought I could do something to help, so much the better, for then I could feel I was being useful, accomplishing something.

I am not a masochist, however. I would never knowingly or willingly tackle the impossible. If I have gotten myself into situations and seen that I was in over my head, I have gotten out. I have only tried to do what I could do and, perhaps more importantly, what I thought was worth doing. I have never been one to be "done for" nor have I allowed anyone to make decisions for me. Whatever choices I have made may have been influenced by my background, but they have been made freely.

So one could look at the fact that I was married and divorced three times and say that I failed in relationships. Certainly it is true that I failed to find a life companion. That I'm sorry about. I do feel I had a lot to share that now will probably never be shared, at least not with a partner. But, at the same time, I realize that until recently I didn't know how to relate to the kind of person who would have been capable of sharing those things with me. I got what I was looking for-- interesting men with brilliant but eccentric minds and emotional problems. They enriched my life greatly, though sometimes nearly at the expense of my sanity.

I would also have to admit that I was not the parent that, in retrospect, I would like to have been. And despite its being a cliché, I would have to say truly that given the lack of meaningful models when I was a child and the various difficulties I had to cope with when my children were little, I perhaps did as well as I could under the circumstances. Though none of my children has accomplished anything spectacular, and although I know they have their various problems from time to time, none of them is a complete failure or social outcast either. They are all fairly normal people. But what is most satisfying for me is the great pleasure I take in knowing them as adults. It was not easy being a parent, especially when the first three were little. But now that they are all grown, their very existence seems like a miracle to me. After all those years of thinking of myself as having no family, I finally have one-- my own children and grandchildren!

As for my so-called "career", one could say that I failed there. It's true I never managed to have a permanent tenured teaching position. In fact the job I held the longest might have become permanent if my disposition had been different. If, when I encountered an authority figure who for her own personal reasons needed to forcefully impose that authority, I had been able to sidestep gracefully instead of fighting what I felt was unfair treatment head on, I might about now be retiring from that position with a secure pension.

But about what I accomplished during my time as a teacher, I have no regrets. I know I gave my best efforts, which I even have the audacity to think were not inconsiderable. (Here you may see the little girl being encouraged by her grandmother to dance expressively across the Oriental carpet.)

I know there were students I reached that would not have been reached otherwise. Oh yes, of course, there were some to whom I was just an average teacher, or worse. But I also feel there are some people out there who are living lives just a little better, more enlightened, more satisfying because of something that happened in that classroom, nothing momentous perhaps, just a light going on, just a glimpse of another way of looking at things, just a slightly different way of approaching life and its problems. If there are even one or two people like that out there, I am satisfied because I know I have made a difference.

I had to take early retirement a few years ago. The stress of shifting from one job to another and being given frustrating assignments in which I could not do my best, on top of the accumulated stress from problem relationships, finally took its toll. I was diagnosed with a rare bleeding disorder that the doctors know little about. There is no known cure and no specific treatment.

Fortunately, after trying some approaches that were worse than the disease and telling me I might soon be minus some internal organs, the doctors have finally come up with something that seems to work. Of course, I can't give them full credit. When it comes to health matters, I am no more inclined to give over control to someone else than I am in any other area of my life.

I have always been a believer in the importance of diet and in "natural" forms of healing. That belief was certainly put to the test this time. I tried everything from Chinese herbs to therapeutic touch and more. And finally a combination of the doctors' approach and my efforts has paid off. I can lead a fairly normal life now, with some restrictions of course.

Now one way to look at this disease business would be to say that it has been a tragedy in my life. But, on the other hand, I have gained greatly from the experience. I have spent enough time in hospitals that they no longer frighten me as they once did. I have some "hospital savvy" now about how to survive in that less than ideal environment. Mind you, I don't plan to spend any more time in them if I can possible help it.

And while my disease was never considered "fatal", there was one night at University Hospital when I really felt I had to come to terms with death. Since then, death has taken on a different meaning for me. I can't say, of course, what I will actually experience when it is closer and more certain. But for now, at least, it has lost its fearful aspect. I see it more as another adventure, probably the greatest one of all with no assurance as to what is on the other side.

Many fear that unknown reality beyond. I can easily understand how it could be frightening, how one could feel alone and isolated when one faces that which all our family security, wealth, or position cannot insulate us from. It is natural to cling to what is known, what is familiar. It's the old security blanket syndrome. But there is also something appealing about approaching the unknown, about starting off on yet another adventure.

When I step inside the circle of stones, it may just be my imagination but time seems to suddenly stand still. Everything stops. My cares and concerns seem insignificant. The colors of the grasses in the meadow, the distant flowers and the trees above intensify. They seem to glow, to shimmer, to radiate a kind of life I only remember experiencing before that day when I took LSD on the beach in Carmel. I felt then that the drug was only enabling me to get a glimpse into something that had always been there but that my senses had been unable to perceive before.

Physicists tell us, of course, that what we see as solid reality is, in fact, only appearance masking the movement of billions of particles through enormous empty space. Deepak

Chopra calls reality "an infinitely ambiguous, ceaselessly flowing quantum soup".

Behind every apparent truth there lies an enormity much more complex than we can possibly perceive because all our experiences from infancy on (and perhaps before) cause us to choose only a limited amount of data, that which is beneficial or useful to us or which fits with previous perceptions. I am not recommending the use of hallucinogenic drugs because I know they have their dangers, but I do value any approach that can show us the limitations of our own particular way of seeing things and make us more accepting of other's perceptions of "reality".

When I walk in Jericho, I feel a great peace and contentment. Particularly when I pause at the circle of stones, I know there is much around me I cannot perceive or understand. But I have lived long enough to trust. If, looking back at the tangled skeins of my life I can now see a pattern and a purpose which were not visible to me before, I trust that whatever has led me to this place will, in its infinite wisdom, take me wherever else I need to go.

Epilogue

This book was completed just before I moved to Salt Spring Island in the fall of 1996. I did some editing, sent some chapters out to publishers and literary agents, and made copies of the book to give to a few friends to review for me. This process took up most of that fall and winter. By spring I had collected a number of polite and encouraging rejection letters from publishers and agents. It took longer to get responses from my friends. When all were finally accounted for, the responses ranged from either pleasantly complimentary, to telling me what I should have thought or felt about someone, to absolutely livid that I could possibly forgive that "pig" Vittorio. Even the fact that it took so long to get some of the copies and responses back seemed to be telling me that what I had written did not exactly qualify as a "page turner". So I put the book away, thinking that after some time had passed I would be able to read what I had written with more objectivity and revise accordingly.

That was almost eight years ago. I have picked up the manuscript a few times over those years, but only in the past few months have I been able to read through the whole book from a fairly objective perspective. Fortunately, one of my friends who read the manuscript had given me some useful feedback on areas that needed clarification. Some passages, where my intent had seemed clear to me before, did need revising. Going through my reviewers' comments, I was still disturbed by some that seemed to indicate that the reader just didn't "get" what I was trying to say, particularly those who failed to understand the importance of compassion and forgiveness. Now, rereading what I wrote, I feel even more strongly that I mean every word, and except for the few passages that needed alteration to make my intended meaning more clear, nothing has been changed.

In those eight years much has happened, and yet all of it seems to fit with the patterns I had described previously in the book. Vittorio died about five years ago in an "accidental" fall from the eighth floor balcony of his apartment in Japan. I would describe his death as "subconscious suicide". When his friend phoned me from Japan to tell me about the accident, I had just awakened from a dream. In the dream I was in a large public sort of room sitting at the end of a long table with Vittorio sitting to my left. There were other people in the room standing with drinks in their hands talking and socializing but not paying any attention to us. Vittorio said nothing but had an expression on his face that I was familiar with but that I doubt most of his friends ever saw, a sort of pout that meant "Don't you feel sorry for me?" My response, again a nonverbal transmission, was the equivalent of "No, I don't feel sorry for you. Pull up your socks and be a man." His friend on the phone told me that he and other friends had just held a sort of "wake" for Vittorio while the cremation process was taking place. It was a social occasion with food, drink, and Bob Dylan records being played. I couldn't help but think that that was where I had just been in my dream. And at that point, yes, I did feel sorry for him.

Not long after Vittorio's death I found out that my half-brother Bill was ill with what was undoubtedly terminal lung cancer. My stepmother, Rose, had died just the year before of the same thing. I had been down to visit her shortly before she died, and Bill had come over to her retirement home for lunch. We had a chance to sit and talk for a while during her nap. It was fascinating to talk to someone I hardly knew and disagreed with on almost every subject and yet at the same time felt such a strong visceral connection to. He phoned to tell me when she died a few months later and we had kept in touch by phone since then. He had what at first appeared to be back problems but it wasn't long before doctors recognized that he had cancer.

It finally reached a point where the doctors were going to let him go home from the hospital because there was nothing further they could do. He was in a wheelchair by that time and needed someone to help him until home care could be arranged. I flew down to LA and rented a car to drive out to his place in Corona, about an hour and a half east of LA.

He was living in an upscale trailer park with security gates. His "mobile home" was a "doublewide" two-bedroom. The living room had one recliner chair, an oversized television, and a desk whose matching chair had an authentic John Wayne gun and holster slung over its side. One wall was covered with a gigantic American flag while on another wall hung a framed certificate of membership in the American Rifle Association. One day Bill was interviewing an applicant for his home care help, a well dressed, seemingly well educated young woman. He was explaining that there was something she should know if she was going to work there. He kept a loaded pistol in the drawer beside his bed. However, he explained, it could only be fired by him having a special ring on his finger, a ring specially made for that purpose. I was expecting her to recoil in horror at this information. Instead she just smiled and said, "What a good idea. I should get something like that for one of my guns".

My brother's connection to right wing attitudes was a bit of a culture shock but not surprising given what I already knew about the family's politics. What did surprise me was his telling me that he had always felt that Dick, his younger brother who had died so early, was the family's, or at least his father's, favorite. It made me think that perhaps when I "disappeared", he had become the scapegoat for the family in my absence. There were also still traces of the old family feeling toward me. When I went out to the store or even to get the mail for him, he seemed not quite sure that I would be able to accomplish the task without some mishap. But I suppose the funniest and most touching revelation was when I was putting away the laundry I had just washed and dried. I had folded his socks and underwear just as I usually do mine at home. I opened the drawer to put them away and found the ones already there folded just the same way. I almost cried at this bit of genetic serendipity!

Bill died a few months after my visit. I had spoken to him just a few days earlier, and he knew it was only a matter of time. His stepdaughter phoned to tell me she had gone over when he failed to answer the phone and found him slumped over on the floor in front of his wheel chair, the TV still blaring. She took care of the cremation and the scattering of ashes he had requested and all the financial matters as he had left everything to her.

When I had gone down there, it was my intention simply to help out until he could get regular hired help. I also hoped for some sort of reconnection with the family through getting to know him better. It wasn't until I had been there a few days that I realized there was a bit of money involved. Despite Rose's telling me that she was leaving all her money to charities, I found that she had left a considerable portion of what was over a million dollar estate to Bill. Then there was whatever his "trailer" house was worth, plus two trucks, a sizable gun collection, retirement plans, etc. He had not yet made a will when I arrived, and I strongly encouraged him to do so. If he had not made a will, I imagine since his brother's son and I were his only surviving relatives, that his estate would have been split between us. However, I felt that it was important for him to decide for himself where the money should go. When his stepdaughter told me he had left everything to her, I have to admit I felt hurt, the same old rejection kind of hurt that I have always felt as a result of that family's attitudes toward me. The money would have been nice, but in this case it really was the thought that counted-- the thought that I was still not considered good enough to be a part of that family was what hurt the most.

Bryan Sr. died a year ago last August after a series of strokes, the last of which left him unable to work in the studio. Bryan Jr., Bekah and David were all there to see him the last day and his fourth wife, Marilyn, was with him until he died peacefully the following morning. It seemed to me that he was willing to keep going even after the first stroke had interfered with his verbal communication skills. But when the last stroke caused a paralysis that would have prevented him from painting, he simply decided to die. And I can't help but think he died peacefully because, at the age of 75, he had done what he set out to do--create a significant body of work that will live on after him. Whether in his lifetime he achieved the recognition or monetary reward he deserved was, for him, really beside the point. The night after he died he came to me in a dream very simply and directly, no setting, nothing extraneous. He was just there asking in a nonverbal way not exactly for what might be called "forgiveness" but rather just checking to see if there were any hard feelings, regrets, anything needing to be resolved between us. I simply told him, no, that there was nothing left to be resolved, and then sent him on his way with the most extraordinarily powerful burst of love

I have ever felt, a burst of love totally beyond any conscious volition on my part.

Regarding the two dreams I have mentioned here, I am only telling what I experienced. Whether you, as reader, choose to accept my interpretation of those dreams will depend, just as your reaction to the rest of my book will depend, on your own beliefs, attitudes, and past experience. As I said at the beginning, it is my belief that there is no single reality but rather a different reality for each individual. I can only hope that some people who take the time to read this book will share enough of my vision to understand and appreciate the absolute amazement and wonder with which I view the life experience.

ISBN 1-41204189-9

9 781412 041898

37150552R00133

Made in the USA
San Bernardino, CA
28 May 2019